D1460635

# West African families in Britain

**Library of Social Work**

General Editor:
Noel Timms
Professor of Social Work Studies
University of Newcastle upon Tyne

# West African families in Britain

## A meeting of two cultures

*edited by*
**June Ellis**
*Department of Social Administration*
*University of Birmingham*

*with contributions by*
June Ellis
Pat Stapleton
Vivien Biggs

**Routledge & Kegan Paul**
London, Henley and Boston

*First published in 1978*
*by Routledge & Kegan Paul Ltd*
*39 Store Street,*
*London WC1E 7DD,*
*Broadway House,*
*Newtown Road,*
*Henley-on-Thames,*
*Oxon RG9 1EN and*
*9 Park Street,*
*Boston, Mass. 02108, USA*
*Set in 10 on 11pt English*
*and printed in Great Britain by*
*The Lavenham Press Ltd*
*Lavenham, Suffolk*


*British Library Cataloguing in Publication Data*

*West African families in Britain.—(Library of social work).*

*1. Africans in Great Britain*
*I.Ellis, June II. Series*
*301.45'19'66041 DA125.W/ 78-40374*

*ISBN 0 7100 8954 6*

# Contents

# Notes on contributors

*June Ellis* took a degree in Social Administration at the University of Birmingham and then spent a year at the University of California before going to West Africa. She taught for five years at the University of Ghana, and she now teaches human growth and behaviour to social work students at Birmingham University.

*Pat Stapleton* has a degree in sociology from LSE. She first lived in West Africa from 1953 to 1959, doing occasional lecturing and research, and was Senior Social Worker with the Commonwealth Students' Children Society in London for eight years. Since 1971 she has spent extended periods back in West Africa. She is currently Assistant Director of the UK Committee for UNICEF.

*Vivien Biggs* studied at LSE and has a Certificate in Social Science. She has spent a total of ten years in Africa, for most of that time working with her husband for Save the Children Fund in Lesotho. Afterwards she worked for the Commonwealth Students' Children Society for nine years, initially as a social worker and latterly as Liaison and Information Officer, and she has recently taken up an appointment with the Church of England Children's Society.

# Acknowledgments

We should like to acknowledge the interest and support of Mr B. B. Boateng, General Secretary of the Commonwealth Students' Children Society, and of members of his staff, and we are especially grateful for permission to use material from the files of the Society in the case histories which were written by Pat Stapleton and Vivien Biggs. We are also very grateful to Mr Peter Tucker, Chief Executive of the Commission for Racial Equality, who was involved in the preparation of material on the legal aspects, and participation in discussions of the manuscript. We thank the Editor of *The Times* for allowing us to quote from *The Times* 'law reports', and the Editor of *Social Work Today* for permission to use material originally published in that journal. Many others have contributed: our husbands have 'lived' with the book, and have helped to shape the ideas, as well as providing encouragement and criticism. Mrs Joyce Rimmer made many valuable suggestions, and Mr John Cypher made helpful comments on Chapter six. Others, too numerous to mention, should be thanked for their advice and special thanks must go to Miss Mercia Pee and to Mrs Valerie Matthews for their secretarial help.

Although each of the writers of the book has taken responsibility for particular chapters, writing it has been very much a joint venture, and we have discussed and shared ideas throughout.

Finally, our grateful thanks must go to all those West Africans who have so generously shared their family life with us, both in Britain and in West Africa, and from whom we have learnt so much.

Chapter One

# Introduction

*June Ellis*

## Introduction

Ours is a multi-racial society. It is also prejudiced, with a low level of understanding of ethnic minorities. One group, the focus of this book, whose distinctive culture is little appreciated in Britain, comes from West Africa and is largely made up of students and their children. Though this group is small compared with those from Asia and the Caribbean, their social work needs are considerable and they are not being adequately met. West Africans are often confused with West Indians and in talking to them it is apparent that many are disappointed by the ignorance about West Africa that they encounter in Britain and by what they see as a widespread lack of interest in their countries.

The sheer scale of West Africa is not generally appreciated in Britain; it is an area that is larger than Europe. There is considerable variation in climate and vegetation, the rain forest near the coast giving way further north to grasslands and scrub, and eventually, on the fringes of the Sahara, to an absence of permanent vegetation. Relatively few people live in these northern territories but further south, and especially towards the coast, are large heavily populated urban areas. There are many different tribes and languages, and the Islamic and Christian faiths flourish alongside the traditional religion.

The countries of West Africa are of relatively recent origin, their political boundaries in many cases reflecting the fortunes of former colonial powers and sometimes cutting across the older tribal groupings (see map, p. 2). We shall mainly be concerned with Nigeria and Ghana, the two West African countries from which most of the students in Britain come, though we shall also refer to other countries, particularly Sierra Leone. It was as these countries

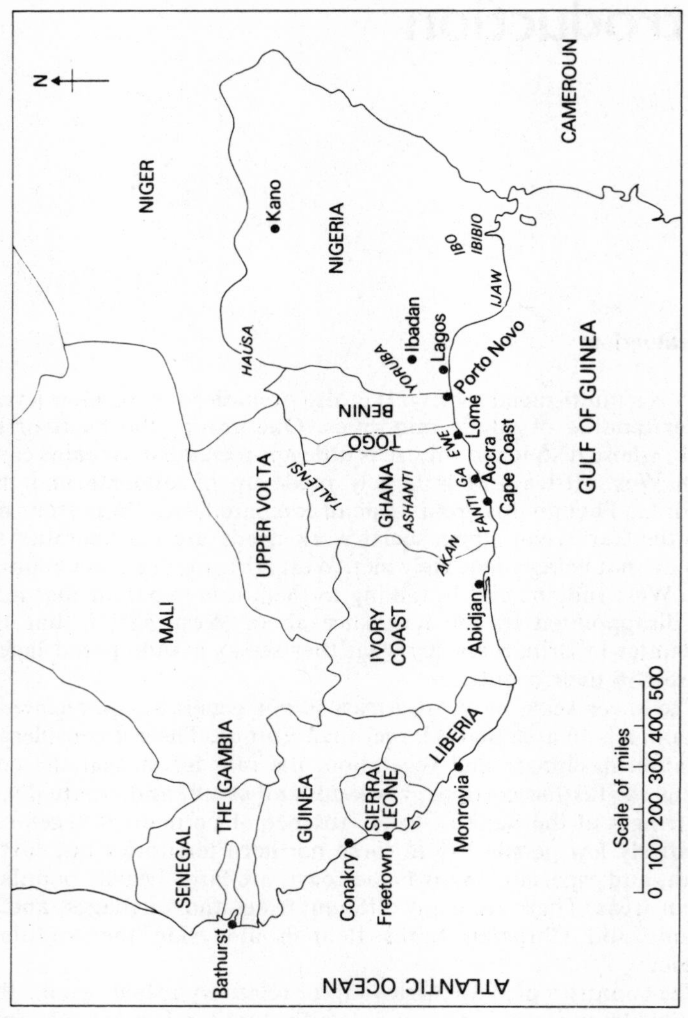


*Figure 1* West Africa indicating some of the principal peoples.

gained their independence in the late 1950s and early 1960s that the number of students coming to Britain assumed substantial proportions. Most West Africans come planning to stay for only a few years to pursue a particular educational goal and then return to their own countries. Often the problems they meet are such that they take longer than anticipated to gain qualifications, but in general they are short-stay residents with a particular aim in view. Many are married and have families with them and it is problems that arise in connection with the care of the children that are the main source of their social work needs. Bewildered by the complexity of the British social services, West African parents are surprised and puzzled at the responses of British social workers to their enquiries about provisions. The inadequacy of day-care facilities, difficulties over accommodation, and the desire by both husband and wife to make the best possible use of their time in Britain, such as will be described in subsequent chapters, mean that parents commonly make use of fostering for their children. Local authorities are understandably reluctant to take children with parents to look after them into care and so private fostering, with all its disadvantages, may appear the only option. It has been estimated that there are about 6,000 West African children in private foster homes in Britain and they probably constitute a majority of all privately fostered children.[1]

The low priority generally given to work with children who are privately fostered[2] is partly due to the many pressures on local authority social workers and also to the discretionary nature of the regulations governing private fostering which are very different from the precise, statutory obligations which relate to children fostered by the local authority. However, an important additional factor in the neglect of privately fostered children who are West African is the lack of understanding of their culture by most British social workers. They find it hard to appreciate why West African parents should want to foster; after all they could look after their children themselves; the mothers do not have to work. As one social worker remarked, and this is by no means an uncommon reaction, 'According to *any* standards these parents are irresponsible.' Clearly it is hard to imagine a worker with such a judgmental approach being able to communicate sympathetically with a West African mother who wishes to place her child in a foster home. Even a social worker who does not take this hard line would find it very difficult to act as a mediator between foster parent and natural parent without an appreciation of the differences in approach to children and child-training that there are in West Africa and Britain, and of the contrasting and perhaps conflicting expectations of fostering that are associated with these.

The need for a book such as this became apparent at the international seminar on the West African child in Britain, held in Nigeria early in 1975 and organized jointly by the Commonwealth Students' Children Society and the Sociology Department of the University of Ibadan in Nigeria. In the following chapters many of the issues raised at the seminar will be discussed. The passing of the Children Act later in 1975 has made a deeper understanding of West Africans even more important, for the Act empowers the Secretary of State to draw up regulations to govern private fostering which, when they are implemented, will require a greater statutory involvement of social workers with West Africans; and the strengthening of the position of foster parents, by the Act, which is likely to lead to an increase in the number of custody disputes involving West African children (we shall be discussing the difficult issues raised by these) will mean that social workers will have a crucial role to play in relation to the courts.

In this book, we have set out to give an account of the many difficulties experienced by West Africans in Britain and, through an examination of aspects of traditional African society and culture, to provide a framework for greater understanding. We hope to go some way towards enabling readers to enter with imagination and sympathy into a view of the world that is different from their own: to see things through African eyes.

Of course, we cannot hope, in a book of this sort and of this length, to do justice to the varieties of practice that exist in West Africa and readers who wish to learn more of the culture should follow the suggestions for further reading given at the end of the book. Whilst not wishing to deny the diversity that undoubtedly exists, we still think it is possible to speak of an African world view. Darryl Forde, the anthropologist, puts our position,[3]

> There can . . . be no single 'blue-print' that will apply directly to all African cultures and there is correspondingly no short way to the understanding of particular peoples. There are however, recurrent themes and a number of main patterns of activity and interconnections which are valuable guides to this understanding.

It is with some of these recurring themes, which predate and transcend many national boundaries, that we shall be concerned in subsequent chapters, particularly with an eye to drawing contrasts between West Africa and Britain. Although our sources are mainly Nigerian and Ghanaian (as also are most of the West African students in Britain) it is likely that what is written about Nigeria and Ghana applies substantially to other West African states, at least in the areas that concern us.

## African myths

We have all in Britain been exposed to the traditional view of Africa as the Dark Continent. Africa has been characterized as primitive and savage, and as a place of ignorance, darkness and death. Even as far back as the eighteenth century there are images that are still quite recognizable today. It has been pointed out that Defoe in *The Life, Adventures and Piracies of the Famous Captain Singleton* 'embodies most of the stereotypes which were to characterize later European writing on Africa—the irrationality and the gullibility of the African who would barter food, cattle and other necessities for a few pieces of European iron and silver frippery; the poverty of Africa's material culture (often equated with the absence of a civilization); the fabulous wealth of the continent waiting to be exploited by the resourceful Europeans; the fear of the white man's might . . . all this supporting that unbridled paternalism, the sense of the "civilizing mission" of the white man, which reached its full development during the Victorian age'.[4]

More modern writers, for instance Joseph Conrad, Joyce Cary and Graham Greene, whilst not caricaturing the African so obviously, have, by choosing Africa as a setting for exploring man's 'baser instincts', contributed to a demeaning view of African culture.[5]

A second myth about Africa is the obverse of the first; Africa is seen in positive, almost glowing, terms as a place of sweetness and light. Going back at least to Rousseau's idea of the 'noble savage', it has a particular appeal at a time when we are increasingly aware of the shortcomings of modern industrial society in the West with its complexity, its impersonality, its loneliness and lack of meaning. To dislocated 'one-dimensional man', Africa, with its seemingly simpler, more wholesome, way of life may seem to represent some kind of panacea. In a recent book about Africa, the distinguished anthropologist, Colin Turnbull, does not entirely avoid this trap although his book is well worth reading for the picture it gives of traditional societies as dignified and as sharing an underlying unity.[6]

## Another view

A romantic view of traditional Africa is no nearer the truth than the patronizing one already referred to. An honest assessment must recognize that the traditional life has its weaknesses as well as its strengths but—and this is important and was not much appreciated by early missionaries and colonists—it has a meaning and coherence of its own and is certainly not an inferior version of our culture. Government and law were not brought by the white man, nor religion by the missionaries. Viewed on its own premises, the traditional life has validity, and it is a way of life from which we may learn; though not without difficulty.[7]

It has been rightly pointed out that 'every way of seeing is also a way of not seeing':[8] we in the West are steeped in a culture where the individual is valued highly and where to regard man as other than an end in himself is considered undesirable. It therefore takes a great effort, emotional as well as intellectual, to begin to appreciate a society, such as that of West Africa, where the individual has counted for little and where the welfare of one is always thought to be subordinate to the general good. It is vital, if we wish to understand West African culture (and the attitudes of West African students in Britain) that we should grasp the different relationship that exists between society and the individual. The emphasis that is placed on the public good there, and the consequent de-emphasis of the individual, is probably the most important difference between the two societies and is the key to the many differences in attitude and approach that are to be found.

Associated with the idea of the importance of the individual are a number of other notions that are logically and conceptually related and that are at the heart of our thinking about what is important and worth while: autonomy, self-development, individual happiness and privacy. We regard a mature morality as one in which the individual reflects and chooses and does not simply behave according to custom, or in obedience to authority, or because of conformity to his peers. The idea of autonomy is important in social work not only as a goal of training—we seek to encourage it in students—but also because we assume the potential for autonomy in our clients and strive to enhance their ability to choose for themselves.

If we consider privacy, another of these associated values, it is clear that we also attach great importance to it. We know that 'an Englishman's home is his castle' and that the English take a pride in keeping themselves to themselves (to such an extent that the British government has had to mount a Good Neighbour Campaign!). It has been suggested that privacy is a prerequisite of mental health, and an important element in the Christian religion is the idea of a very private relationship with God.

It is very different in West Africa. In traditional society, man is not man on his own; the individual gains his significance from and through his relationships with others: religion is collective rather than private; art represents universals rather than individual experience. A commentator on the West African novel makes a point that has a more general relevance, expressing very well the relationship between the individual and the community:[9]

> the West African novel tends to show the individual characters not through their private psychological experiences, but through

community and social life and activities of a collective or general nature, with individual sentiments and actions deriving force and logic from those of the community.

Anyone who wishes to appreciate traditional African society and culture can in fact do no better than start to read the novel *Things Fall Apart* by Chinua Achebe, an Ibo writer from Nigeria.[10] In this book, which is a major literary work, Achebe portrays the strengths and rhythms of the collective life with its dignity, its sense of harmony and its traditional mechanisms for dealing with disputes. What emerges is a rounded picture, and one in which the individual is very firmly placed in his universe, with his relationships to others clearly defined. But Achebe is uncompromisingly honest in his writing and he conveys also the harshness and the individual suffering that are part of traditional life and the way in which someone who deviates must be sacrificed to the interests of society, for an offence is an offence against society. Achebe shows the appeal of Christianity, with its emphasis on individual salvation, to the misfits of traditional society and, through his central character, who offends against the community, he underlines the fearful impact of ostracism.

Clearly this is a society in which the ideas that have been suggested as important in British society have little place and indeed are counter-valued: autonomy, in so far as it represents a challenge to custom and authority, is regarded as a threat, and the development of the 'mobile self', and notions of individual happiness and privacy have little place. These differences present the British social worker with the challenging task of seeking to reconcile what, in the Western tradition, have come to be regarded as important social work values, with the values of a West African client that are likely to reflect a different set of priorities.

## The old and the new

Undoubtedly all African cultures have been exposed to Western influences, the effects of which should not be underplayed, but despite these there are grounds for supposing that the old traditional ways have a continuing relevance, along with the new. It is important to explore this at some length because it is central to much of the book.

Most people in West Africa are born in the village and, it may be argued, they 'carry' the village with them for the remainder of their lives. Tetteh, writing of those Ghanaians who have moved from the rural areas to the towns, points out that,[11]

> the urbanite still has strong loyalties to his extended family

> and keeps contact with its members . . . Most extended families also have shrines of their ancestors, and even highly educated and high status persons come to these shrines to ask for the blessing of the ancestors in any important projects they want to undertake. If a man is going abroad he pours libation to his ancestors to ask them to protect him in foreign lands.

Obiechina, a Nigerian writer, describes the extent to which intellectuals remain 'rooted' in the traditional culture:[12]

> Even among middle-class professional university educated West Africans who have been most intensely subjected to Western acculturation a large body of traditional thinking still exists . . . the average town dweller in West Africa . . . is still a peasant at heart, with a thin layer of modern sophistication concealing the deep centre of traditional beliefs and feelings.

Thus, when a West African is ill he is likely to make use of the traditional healer as well as the doctor[13] and a professional scientist may also inhabit a world where a different kind of logic prevails, and where the lines between the natural and the supernatural, the physical and the metaphysical, are not clearly drawn. This mingling and co-existence of different kinds of reality in West Africa is discussed by Baeta: 'So vivid is the sense of the supernatural or spiritual world that its distinction is not always clearly present to the common awareness.'[14] It is powerfully evoked in the strangely surrealist writings of Amos Tutuola,[15] and it is exemplified in traditional West African religion where the lines between the living and the dead are blurred, and the ancestors are conceived of as continuing spiritual presences watching over and admonishing their living descendants: 'The dead are not alive but they do exist.'[16]

The only true death in West Africa is when a man has no one to remember him and to perform the traditional ceremonies on his behalf (and, as will be seen later, this is an important part of the great desire for children found in West Africa). The horror of such a situation is vividly conveyed by Achebe in *Things Fall Apart* when Okonkwo, the central character, hears of his son Nwoye's conversion to Christianity with its threat of death to the ancestors: 'a terrible prospect, like the prospect of annihilation'.[17] Of course it could well be that this would remain no more than a threat, for conversion to Christianity would not necessarily mean abandonment of the traditional practices. The traditional culture is pluralistic and extraordinarily accommodating and religious toleration is a strong feature of West African life: 'Christians and Muslims . . . have recourse to the traditional sorcerer's magical help . . . while some Christians would pour libation to the ancestral spirits or be present at strictly animist ceremonies and customary rituals, especially on tribal or family occasions.'[18] Interestingly enough (and this makes the point very well about the tenacity of the old beliefs) in a later novel by Achebe, *No Longer at Ease*, this same convert to Christianity, Nwoye, who had become a Christian catechist, opposes his *own* son's proposed marriage on purely traditional grounds that are quite inconsistent with Christian beliefs: Clara, the girl his son loves is beautiful and educated, but she is 'osu', that is, a descendant of a slave class, and in tribal law such a marriage between slave and free would be taboo. But the irony is even greater than it appears, for 'osu' are cult-slaves deriving their status from traditional Ibo religion![19]

It seems then that the old ways remain, and it is likely that they will be especially significant for those areas of life that are so central and important, those concerned with family and children. A Nigerian has no doubts on this score after undertaking a survey. Traditional beliefs persist despite social change and urban residence and of child-training in Nigeria he notes that there are 'little or no urban-rural differences because of the close village ties of city dwellers'. 'Living in the city will certainly change some of his values and beliefs but such a change will, by and large, affect his attitudes towards fads and fashions . . . .' He argues that the traditional values, mores and folkways persist for, 'Beliefs about child rearing are usually bound up with beliefs about life itself. They are culturally transmitted and culturally learned. They are held without question.'[20]

## Education

Since it is the search for education that has led to the presence of substantial numbers of West Africans in Britain, it is appropriate to look briefly at the impact of Western education on traditional society, and to indicate its importance in West Africa.

In the traditional world, education and socialization were synonymous. There were no specialized educational institutions, and the society itself was educative. As Hurd has pointed out, this kind of education was quite adequate in a relatively simple, unchanging society, and early European attempts to provide schools in West Africa met with notably little interest except along the coastal fringe.[21] A quotation from the Asantahene (Ashanti king) in 1876 nicely encapsulates the traditional view: 'Ashantee children have better work to do than to sit down all day idly to learn . . . . They have to fan their parents, and do other work which is better.'[22]

From very early days, however, schools had occasionally been established in the trading posts along the coast (the first recorded school was in 1529) but they tended to be short-lived.[23] And West

African students in Britain are a phenomenon dating back at least to the eighteenth century. One of these was Philip Quaque who spent eleven years in England and in 1765 became the first African ordained as a priest of the Church of England. He returned to West Africa where he established a school at Cape Coast and spent fifty years working as 'Missionary, Catechist and Schoolmaster to the Negroes on the Gold Coast'.[24]

The combination of roles assigned to Philip Quaque is significant, for a major impetus in education in the early days was religious and, throughout the nineteenth century, mission schools were opened in the West African territories. It has been suggested that this activity is partly to be explained by a desire on the part of Europeans to make up for the injustices of slavery and for the part they had played in the slave trade.[25] The motives that gave rise to this desire to show a 'better' side of European civilization were more acceptable than some of the assumptions underlying them; assumptions—not surprising in their historical context—of the superiority of the white man and his civilization. The following quotation is revealing:[26]

> Everyday life in Cape Coast took on the colour of the Victorian era. The School Assembly Hall would echo one evening to the resolutions passed by the local branch of the Society for the Prevention of Cruelty to Animals; the next it would be filled with an enthusiastic audience treated to a magic lantern lecture on the Stately Homes of England . . . . Beaton's 'Complete Etiquette for English Gentlemen' sold at the Bookshop. English clothing and English names were postulates of the Christian life. It was undoubtedly an English kingdom of God that the Cape Coast prophets looked forward to.

It was all too easy for pupils to learn not only the rudiments of reading and writing but to accept their own culture as inferior. Chinua Achebe had something to say about this, many years later in a radio interview, 'We have been subjected—we have subjected ourselves too—to this period during which we have accepted everything alien as good and practically everything local or native as inferior.'[27] But there have been far-reaching changes. Few West Africans today are ready to espouse uncritically all that Europe has to offer, nor to be so apologetic about their own culture. There is a new confidence and an insistence on the value and authenticity of their own ways.

The recognition that the flavour and much of the content of European schooling was inappropriate has not been associated with any lessening in enthusiasm for education. For although progress was slow away from the coast (and strong regional inequalities remain) this century has seen the growth of a broadly based enthusiasm for schooling and a corresponding educational expansion. There is no mistaking the intense interest in education and appreciation of its importance that exists now.

Those who have lived in West Africa in recent years cannot but be aware of this. It is commonplace to be approached by eager boys who wish to do jobs in return for payment of school fees or for help in buying school books or uniform. These boys realize the crucial importance of education in a society where differentials are greater than in Britain and the opportunities for advancement outside the formal education system, few. They are encouraged by the example of others, very like themselves, perhaps members of their own family, who have become 'big men'. But it is not just a matter of personal success. Given the emphasis on generosity and on responsibility for one's kin, success for one is felt by many, in a kind of chain of advancement. Those who succeed do so with the help of others and, in return expect to give help, showing little resentment of this, and possibly giving financial support to many people outside their immediate nuclear family.[28] The expectations and the family pressures that West African students coming to Britain experience are captured exactly in the words that follow:[29]

> the letter first brought me the congratulations of my father and all my family on my success. Then my father went on to remind me that I had now started to climb a palm tree which was high and difficult to climb; that many were watching my progress, and much ripe fruit was awaiting me on the successful conclusion of my climb. He ended with the warning that if I failed to reach the top, those watching me, both living and dead, would curse me for failing them. On the other hand, if I reached the top in order simply to gorge myself with fruit, I would surely become sick and fall to the ground and die. But if I returned to my people to share with them the fruit of my labours, then all would sing to my praise and thank me and honour those who had brought me to life.

## Notes

1 Estimate by the Commonwealth Students' Children Society. No official figures on private fosterings have been published since 1969.

2 R. Holman, *Trading in Children,* Routledge & Kegan Paul, 1973. This study which was carried out in the Midlands and which is the only major investigation of private fostering revealed a consistently lower level of supervision of private foster children as compared with those placed by the local authority.

3 C. D. Forde (ed.), *African Worlds: Studies in the Cosmological Ideas and Social Values of African Peoples,* Oxford University Press, 1963, p. xvii.

4 E. Obiechina, *Culture, Tradition and Society in the West African Novel,* Cambridge University Press, 1975, pp. 18-19.

5 Ibid. See pp. 18-25 for a most interesting discussion of foreigners, writing with varying degrees of success, about West Africa.

6 C. T. Turnbull, *Man in Africa,* Newton Abbot, David & Charles, 1976.

7 Mary Kingsley, the famous Victorian traveller, was unusual in her sympathetic understanding of West African life and culture and her books are vivid and interesting. See for instance, M. Kingsley, *Travels in West Africa,* Cass, 1965, 3rd edn.

8 S. Lukes, *Individualism,* Oxford, Basil Blackwell, 1973, p. 149. The discussion that follows owes a good deal to Lukes's book.

9 Obiechina, op. cit., p. 36.

10 C. Achebe, *Things Fall Apart,* London, Heinemann, 1958.

11 P. A. Tetteh, 'Marriage, Family and Household', in W. Birmingham *et al.* (eds), *A Study of Contemporary Ghana,* vol. 2, Allen & Unwin, 1967, p. 215.

12 Obiechina, op. cit., pp. 37 and 40.

13 U. Maclean, *Magical Medicine: A Nigerian Case-Study,* Allen Lane, The Penguin Press, 1971. A fascinating account of the way in which traditional practices and modern European medicine exist side by side, suggesting that traditional medicine gives meaningful answers to questions about the 'whole man' that are in danger of being lost sight of in the Western concentration on 'accurate diagnosis and specific cure'.

14 C. G. Baeta, 'Aspects of Religion', in Birmingham, ed., op. cit., pp. 241-2.

15 '. . . a brief, thronged grisly and bewitching story . . . Nothing is too prodigious or too trivial to put down in this tall devilish story' is how Dylan Thomas described Tutuola's most famous book *The Palm-Wine Drinkard,* Faber & Faber, 1952. To the Western reader the recurring juxtaposition of the mundane and the extraordinary gives the book a strange dreamlike quality. For instance, the search for Death who is known to live in the Dead's town ends when he is encountered 'in his yam garden'.

16 J. Jahn, *Muntu,* Faber & Faber, 1961, p. 108.

17 Achebe, op. cit., p. 139.

18 Baeta, in Birmingham, ed., op. cit., p. 240.

19 C. Achebe, *No Longer at Ease,* Heinemann, 1960.

20 N. Uka, *Growing up in Nigerian Culture,* Ibadan University Press, 1966, p. 29.

21 G. Hurd, 'Education', in Birmingham, ed., op. cit., p. 217.

22 Ibid., pp. 218-19.

23 H. O. A. McWilliam, *The Development of Education in Ghana,* Accra, Longmans, 1964, pp. 8-16.

24 Ibid., p. 11.

25 J. D. Fage, *An Introduction to the History of West Africa,* Cambridge University Press, 1962, 3rd edn, pp. 104-5.

26 E. W. Smith, *Aggrey of Africa,* SCM Press, 1929, p. xl, quoted in McWilliam, op. cit., p. 22.

27 C. Achebe interviewed by Donatus Nwoga, in *African Writers Talking,* ed. D. Duerden and C. Pieterse, Heinemann, 1975, pp. 7-8.

28 J. C. Caldwell, 'Population: General Characteristics', in Birmingham, ed., op. cit., p. 74. He comments that 'two-thirds of university students expect to spend between 10 per cent and 30 per cent of their professional incomes on relatives other than their wives and children'.

29 W. Conton, *The African,* Heinemann, 1960, pp. 21-2.

Chapter Two

# The West African background

*Pat Stapleton*

He that has a brother must hold him to his heart,
For a kinsman cannot be bought in the market,
Neither is a brother bought with money.

(Chinua Achebe, *The Song of the Heart*)

**Introduction**

West Africa is a land of extremes which jostle together and somehow seem to find their own equilibrium; the very rich get richer whilst beggars sleep on the streets and the subsistence farmer scratches a living. The big cities have modern buildings with every facility, but you may still arrive at a first class hotel to find there is no electricity or water on that particular day. You may live in a three storey house, in a modern bungalow or in one made of mud with a 'pan' roof. One day a man will be wearing an immaculate English suit yet the next time you may see him in pink lace or in handwoven cloth. Traffic jams in Lagos can delay you for hours, and much of your shopping can be done from the car whilst waiting to move, but the majority of the population still trek from place to place on foot or by bicycle, although the taxi is more common than the bus, and children who may never have seen a train will grow up quite familiar with the aeroplane. The PhD may have illiterate parents; the subsistence farmer may have children studying in Britain. Christianity and Islam are flourishing in peaceful co-existence; the churches and mosques are crowded, but traditional beliefs are still upheld and the old gods are not forgotten. Modern hospitals and the most up-to-date treatments are available in the cities, but many will still put their faith in the traditional healers. You can find examples of the highest standard and the lowest—in one sense everything is true, and each individual tends to find what he is looking for!

This rich diversity makes generalization extremely difficult, not to say dangerous. There is immense variety within Nigeria alone, with its population estimated at around eighty million, and its diverse peoples, with as much or more to divide them as many of the peoples of Europe, yet often we refer to Africa and Africans as if this huge continent could be easily contained. Some shorthand is however necessary; one needs to take an overall view and it is no doubt true that the factors in common between the different peoples of West Africa are sufficiently strong to justify a general description that can be accepted as valid.

One could argue that it is not so much the difference in tribe or nationality that distinguishes the life styles of individuals, but the occupational circle to which they belong. The university campuses at Ibadan, Accra and Freetown have many similarities as does the senior civil service housing or the army officers' mess in each country. Above all, it is the entry into that circle, commonly referred to as the élite group, which provides the key to a comfortable existence (although frequently an extremely hardworking one), complete with subsidized government housing, car allowance, overseas travel and so on; and the way into this charmed circle is very clearly through education rather than through birth or even wealth. Despite its pejorative overtones in general English usage, I shall use the word 'élite' to describe the western educated group who man the civil service, and the professions, and hold the political power as Lloyd points out:[1]

> The term elite used so commonly today is convenient because it suggests the superior status of its members; it connotes too, positions of influence, which the educated African certainly holds in re-defining traditional values. Furthermore, an elite is thought of as an open group, access to which is not restricted by birth or family antecedents.

It is impossible to give a sound sociological analysis of West African social structure in a few pages. Those who wish to learn more may find that the reading of African novels, of which there are now a substantial number available from West Africa, will give them as much, if not more, insight, with considerably greater pleasure, than academic study. This chapter is merely an attempt to give a general impression of traditional family life and attitudes and the changes that have taken place in recent years, highlighting where possible those aspects that may lead to misunderstandings when West Africans are living in Britain.

The nuclear family is something we take so much for granted as the norm that we may be hindered from seeing its negative aspects. At a time when marriage and the family are being seriously criticized, and an increasing number of the younger generation are looking for some sort of alternative to our highly competitive and individualistic society, perhaps we can learn something from the more open, community-oriented societies of Africa, before they themselves have been too greatly changed by the embrace of western 'development'.

## The family

'I have many mothers', said a Ghanaian doctor during a discussion on family relationships, crystallizing in a few words the difference between the western style, closed, nuclear family, where the concentration of relationships is between husband, wife and children, and the far more open, traditional, extended family, still the norm in West Africa in spite of inevitable changes resulting from the pressures of modern urban living and the impact of western technology.

The family is not easy to define: in one sense the word can be used to include all persons, living or dead, with a common ancestor, but generally the term 'extended family' refers to 'a group of closely related people, known by a common name and consisting usually of a man and his wives and children, his sons' wives and children, his brothers and half-brothers and their wives and children, and probably other near relations', all of whom are bound to each other by ties of mutual obligation.[2] It requires some effort of imagination to understand what it means to be at the centre of such a network with all its duties and responsibilities as well as its privileges. Europeans often feel deceived when an African introduces his 'brother' and it is only later realized that he is not a biological brother. This term is not restricted to that conveyed by 'same mother, same father'. It can include cousins and other distant connections of the same generation, as well as being loosely used to refer to anyone of approximately the same age group from his home area. The term is meaningful and conveys an obligation to treat the man as a brother, however distant the relationship.

Equally, a child may grow up calling her aunt or grandmother 'mother', and regarding her as such because she is the woman with whom she has been most closely brought up, or merely as a term of affection and respect to her mother's relatives. She will of course be aware of her biological mother, but the title can freely be given to a number of women without causing any confusion. (The social worker who is told, 'you are my mother' should accept this as the compliment intended without worrying unduly about dependency.)

Among the Yoruba people of Western Nigeria, kinship extends to all those who can be traced by blood on both the paternal and maternal side, and kinship by marriage extends to the most distant kinsfolk of the spouse. 'To the Yoruba the larger the circle of one's kin, the greater one's social and political importance.'[3] In spite of this complexity it is relevant to note that relationships are described primarily in terms of seniority and there are only five root words in Yoruba to denote relationships: 'baba'—father, 'iya'—mother, 'omo'—child are the three for which one can find an English equivalent; the other two signify relatives born either before or after the individual concerned. This terminology, where one word can refer to, for instance, father, grandfather or uncle does not mean that relationships are not clearly understood—'given any member of the family, the Yoruba can define his exact relationship in general terms and without the use of proper names.'[4] However it is noteworthy that even very fluent English speakers will often transpose personal pronouns, most frequently using 'she' for either sex, and this should not be interpreted as a sign of confusion.

Kinship and seniority can thus be seen as the basic stabilizing elements in traditional societies. 'Kinship ensures loyalty, co-operation, mutual help and mutual tolerance, and seniority guarantees obedience to authority.'[5]

### *Seniority*

The significance of seniority is learnt from infancy, and a child will invariably learn obedience to his older siblings who in turn will readily accept responsibility for the younger one. Child-minders in Britain frequently comment on the strong bonds between siblings, the obedience of the younger one and caring responsibility of the older, even when speaking of two- and four-year-olds. A man in his thirties will feel it normal to seek the advice of father, uncle or senior brother, when making major decisions, and the need for consultation should not be interpreted as an indication of weakness. The idea that a young person can teach an older one is alien, and today inevitably produces tensions in many areas of life where the educated young will find themselves teaching modern techniques to members of their parents' generation. Such attitudes easily produce conflicts with social workers in Britain; for example most African parents when looking for a foster mother, are very distrustful of young women—'what does she know about children when she has not even finished bringing up her own?'—and they may prefer to seek out a grandmother figure often regarded as far too old by the social worker. The young social worker herself, particularly if she is childless, will not readily be regarded as someone whose advice is of great significance.

The importance of respect for older people in African society cannot be overemphasized, and there is a myth, accepted by many West Africans, of all elderly parents in our society being abandoned in old people's homes. They find it reprehensible not to give first priority to the care of their mothers and fathers. The wisdom of the older generation is something that is still valued by go-ahead, westernized young men and women and their advice is often sadly missed when difficult decisions have to be made away from home. 'He may be illiterate but he is very wise' could describe many of the older generation, and this wisdom has been partly acquired by the whole process of open discussion and the resolution of problems that was an integral part of traditional life. Disputes were, and often still are, resolved in public, with the elders present, and in this way an ability to assess situations and understand human behaviour becomes a skill acquired through experience rather than through formal learning. The emphasis in resolving conflicts is usually on finding a workable solution rather than on proclaiming guilt or innocence, and decisions made in public are thus realistic and usually obeyed.

However alien it may seem to our society, with its emphasis both on youth and on individual freedom, understanding the significance of respect for one's elders is one of the keys to the understanding of African societies. The young, well-educated, well-dressed woman who kneels to her elders, and the young graduate who prostrates to his old illiterate mother, are showing respect without the subservience that such behaviour would convey to the British.[6] Another indicator of respect, common throughout West Africa, is a lowering of the eyes. To a European this indicates shiftiness: 'She never looks me straight in the eye' is the usual complaint. Of course she does not, because any well-brought-up girl will lower her eyes when speaking to her elders, and a habit one has been trained in from infancy is hard to break. 'Raising one's eyes to an elderly person constitutes a definite category of offence among the Yoruba.'[7]

## Marriage

Given the complexities and importance of kinship ties, it will easily be understood that marriage is not simply the union of two individuals, but is the joining together of two families, primarily for the purposes of procreation and the continuance of the lineage rather than for personal fulfilment and mutual support. Romantic love is not a traditional concept.

There are basically two types of marriage throughout West Africa: monogamous marriage based on statutory law (which is similar to British law) and polygamous marriage based on customary law (which varies not only from one country to another but within a country from one locality to another). The common feature is that a man has the right to take as many wives as he pleases, except under Islamic law when he may not have more than four.

In traditional society, marriages might be arranged between families when the children were still very young, and a marriage could be enforced against the wishes of either partner. This is rare today although, under Islamic law, a father still has the right to conclude marriages on behalf of his infant sons or daughters. Usually, once a boy has expressed an interest in a certain girl, the parents of both parties have to satisfy themselves as to the suitability of the family into which their child is proposing to marry. They investigate the general social standing and reputation of the family within the community, and such matters as illness, mental disorder, infertility and criminal history. Once agreement has been reached, gifts are exchanged, and various traditional ceremonies are carried out before the bride joins her family.[8] The girl is handed over, not only to the husband, but to his whole family. They become responsible for her well-being and for sorting out any quarrels that may arise. If a husband deserts his wife, she is allowed to remain within the family home as a member of the household so long as she has not offended other members of the family. If her husband dies, she can, if she wishes, remain and marry another member of the husband's family, usually a brother, although it could be a son by another wife. Since her position there depends to a great extent on her children, who have the sole right of inheritance from their father, a widow, if childless, usually returns to her own family and remarries. Such a system ensures that a woman and her children are never left unsupported as the result of death or desertion. This was clearly brought home to me by a student who explained that he was not married although he had a wife. By this he meant that he had inherited the responsibility for his dead brother's wife, and had felt obliged to accept this.

The type of marriage just described is that found in the patrilineal system where inheritance is through the male line as in England, and the wife leaves her family home on marriage to live with her husband. Although this is the commonest pattern it is by no means universal. Among matrilineal peoples, such as the Akan of Ghana, inheritance is through the maternal line and it is from his mother's brothers that a child stands to gain. In these cases the young wife does not necessarily take up residence with her husband, but will visit him regularly at night and prepare his food, whilst remaining in her own family home and bringing up her children there. Of course today many young couples from a matrilineal society will live together, but separate residence is still common. I recently visited a Fanti fishing village on the coast of Ghana where I was shown the separate accommodation belonging to the fishermen who were only visited by their womenfolk. And among the Ga, found mainly around Accra, who combine both systems, people have the right to live in the compound of their parent of the same sex:[9]

> The prevailing residential arrangement in central Accra is that women live with their female relatives and men with their male relatives so that the whole area is a honeycomb of separate male and female compounds. The small children and girls live with their mothers and boys usually go to live with their father somewhere between the ages of six and ten, thus perpetuating the system.

Although the child's relationship with the mother will be very close in the matrilineal system, ties with the father may be much weaker. Many fathers nowadays object to the idea of leaving their wealth to their sister's children rather than to their own, and it seems likely that in time this system will be weakened. Christine Oppong's study of marriage among matrilineal élites in Ghana[10] clearly illustrates the problems for the woman who loses the security of a home with her own mother and siblings and hopes to be provided with a new security by marriage to an educated man. She quotes an Akan husband as saying, 'the modern Akan wife now expects her husband to be a brother as well as lover and father of her children. She looks to him for the permanent home and security she once found with her matrikin.' At the same time the husband's kin will continue to make heavy demands on him, particularly with regard to his sisters and their children. Her study suggests that such demands are the source of the most acute domestic conflicts and struggles.[10]

Although a minority pattern, I have referred to the matrilineal groups at some length because they illustrate the danger of assuming that a genuine family must be living together under one roof. Separate households for man and wife can be perfectly normal and social workers should beware of assuming that if husband and wife are apart there is something wrong with the marriage.[11] The idea of a man training in Birmingham while his wife is a student nurse in Manchester seems perfectly natural, as would the possibility that she might find it just as important to take her brother to visit a child in a foster home as for her husband to visit. Marital problems are of course not ruled out but should not be automatically assumed.

Today most educated young people will make their own choice of marriage partner but they will usually still seek the consent of their parents before marrying. The status and authority of the elders is still widely recognized and family approval is still important. In Sierra Leone 'parents may remind a young person in krio that "okra is never taller than the farmer." In other words a child never escapes from his parents' authority.'[12]

Those studying abroad often meet and marry partners who are not known to their families and this can impose serious strains. Parents who do not support the marriages of their children and who may have other partners in mind for their son or daughter, can often cause breakdown of the marriage. Many young men far from home still feel the need for parental advice, and as a student in his late twenties, much attracted to a girl he met in England, said to me: 'How can I find out about her background? How can I know what she is really like?' He clearly was unable to trust his own judgment. It is still not uncommon for someone studying abroad to ask his parents to arrange a marriage by proxy. The new wife would then come and join her unknown husband in England, often with disastrous consequences.

*Brideprice*

Traditionally the giving of presents, which may include sums of money, at the time of betrothal and on completion of the marriage ceremony, is essential for a valid customary law marriage. To Europeans, the term 'brideprice' is an emotive one that has led to the erroneous conclusion that African women are 'bought'. For this reason many people prefer to use the word 'dowry', the term more commonly reserved for the property that a woman brings into the marriage; as far as I know it has never been suggested that in India and other societies where this is the norm the women are 'buying' their husbands.

The brideprice symbolized the commitment of the boy's family to the marriage, and the acceptance of responsibility on the part of the girl's family to hand her over still a virgin. If the marriage broke down because of self-evident faults on the girl's side, the money would be returned (although this could depend on the number of children she had produced); if the breakdown was caused by the man, the money would be retained, at least until the girl married again, thus providing some form of insurance.

The presentation of gifts such as palm wine, cloth, chickens and goats was partially replaced by money as a result of western influence, and with the expansion of the money economy, the cash contribution increased until abuses became such that legal restrictions were introduced.[13] Whatever legal restrictions exist in the different countries, brideprice today takes a variety of forms. Many couples will abandon the concept completely and educated parents of an educated daughter are unlikely to demand brideprice as such. They will expect to receive some recompense for the money they have spent on her education in the form of the financial contribution that she herself will make in her turn to the education of younger relatives.

Among the Akan of Ghana the handing over of drinks is regarded as the essential feature.[14] The Creoles of Sierra Leone do not approve of the practice but both parties will spend enormous sums on very conspicuous and expensive weddings. In the Gambia today, although this is not formalized, a man is expected to give very expensive presents, such as a watch, a sewing machine and a bed, as engagement presents. These gifts are not usually a contribution to the future household but are frequently kept by the bride's mother. A friend who objected to these increasing demands was telling all his girl friends that he would reserve all presents until after they were married—behaviour not calculated to make him popular with a future mother-in-law.

In some societies, a contribution in the form of labour was also part of the brideprice. Among the Yoruba, a man would be expected to work on his father-in-law's farm, and to help with rebuilding his house, so that a man with many daughters could call on the assistance of many sons-in-law who had a duty to respond. The significance of this today is not so much in terms of manual work but of on-going obligations. Problems arise when a traditional system becomes distorted by external pressures and the normal frame of reference is no longer adequate. The marriage of one student couple in England finally broke down because of the totally unreasonable demands being made by the girl's parents for consumer goods. They shared the common illusion that the streets of London were paved with gold, and initially expected, and received, gifts of a radiogram, followed by a refrigerator and a television set. Their demands became more and more exorbitant until finally they insisted on a car. At this point, the husband, who had tried hard to satisfy them, felt he could go no further; his studies were suffering because of the night job he was doing in order to raise the necessary funds, and he had two small children to provide for. The parents felt he was not honouring his obligations as a son-in-law and they did everything to turn his wife against him. She, torn between these conflicting pressures, had a breakdown and eventually returned to Lagos to her parents, leaving her children with their father.

### *Divorce*

It naturally follows that if marriage is a union of two families rather than of two individuals, divorce also will not be a decision for the couple alone. In fact, as a Nigerian lawyer points out: 'Throughout the duration of the marriage the families are called on at one stage or another to assist the spouses in the settlement of disputes. Often the marriage is continued as the result of sheer family pressures.'[15] On the other hand bad relationships with a member of the other family may sometimes provide grounds for divorce. A husband may, for instance, divorce his wife on the grounds that she is disrespectful to the elders of his family and the family of a married woman may encourage her to leave her husband, because, in view of his conduct towards them, they do not regard him as a good son-in-law.

Failure to produce children would usually be regarded as sufficient grounds for divorce. It is not unknown for a mother to boast that she had finally broken her son's marriage as his wife had not provided the desired grandchildren. This is one of the reasons why, in spite of the difficulties young couples face in Britain when pursuing their studies, they will still feel that the marriage must be sealed with at least one child as soon as possible. Cruelty, mental illness, disease which could affect procreation, as well as persistent adultery would also be grounds for divorce, but it seems that 'customary law puts more emphasis on the fact that a marriage had broken down irretrievably than on the individual responsibility of a spouse for that failure'.[16] Perhaps this is an area where recent changes in British statutory law have brought us closer to African customary law.

A man should not be cruel to his wife and, although he may beat her, relatives or neighbours will intervene if he takes this too far. To understand the reality of this, it needs to be appreciated that there is remarkably little privacy in African family life, even in towns. The climate encourages open living, and life is normally lived on the veranda, in the courtyard or in the communal rooms. It is easy to know when quarrels arise and to gauge the right moment for intervention. This applies equally to the chastisement of children, where it would be usual for a relative to plead for a child once he had been punished sufficiently. The lack of intervention from neighbours in England, resulting from our wish not to be involved in other people's private affairs, can lead to quarrels between West Africans getting out of control, to the point where the police have to be called, in a way that would be inconceivable back home. In marital disputes the advice given by the elders is very directive. When they are not available to settle disagreements, husband or wife may feel at a loss. The following extract from a letter written by an aggravated husband lacking the support of family elders, to the department of social welfare in Freetown, quoted by Harrell-Bond in her study of marriage in Sierra Leone, illustrates a rather different perception of a social worker's role from that in Britain:[17]

> I am making the following complaints against my legal wife:—
> 1. She had from long time neglected cooking in the house at the appropriate time, letting the children to suffer.

2. She does not clean the house and she is more inclined to her self market making, leaving the children abruptly.
3. She does not respect me even in the presence of people or before my fellow men. She gives me open defiance and can't apologise . . . .

Sir I am appealing to you to warn this lady to stop all these malpractices and maltreatments and let us co-operate and work as a team.

*Polygamy*

Polygamous marriages are still very common throughout West Africa even among Christians. A large proportion of students at present in Britain will have been brought up in polygamous households even though they themselves are most likely to contract a monogamous marriage. To the European, polygamy is usually seen either as the subject for a joke or as degrading to women, but in societies where it is the norm for everyone to be married, it does provide every woman with a place in the community. Although today the majority of women, and especially the educated ones, appear to have a strong preference for monogamy,[18] there were undeniable advantages in the polygamous way of life. Given that in many societies sexual intercourse is not approved of during pregnancy and breastfeeding, it provided an institutional framework which discouraged extra-marital relationships. As a child was not usually weaned until the age of two or three, such a system also provided a method of birth control which led to well-spaced families. Babies following each other at yearly intervals are far more frequently found in monogamous families.

In a Yoruba polygamous household each wife has her own room in the family compound and is responsible for the care of her own children as well as sharing duties in relation to the husband. In time of sickness or family crisis, or if she is engaged in some trading or professional training that takes her away from home, children are cared for by other wives. Many women confess that they would rather share a husband in a structured way, with women they know and may even have helped to choose, than unknown rivals who, in a technically monogamous situation, will probably be involved with their husbands. African women seem to accept the 'polygamous' nature of men and would not necessarily expect to live constantly with their husbands as most European wives do or to demand standards of fidelity which they would feel to be hypocritical. In this situation a woman may feel much freer to pursue her own interests and for instance to go abroad and study for several years, leaving the children in the care of co-wives or her own mother.

Perhaps the best insight into the joys and tensions of polygamous households can be obtained from novels; some writers tend to present somewhat idyllic pictures of traditional society, others stress the jealousies and rivalries that arise. As in all marriage patterns there are wide variations. Thus a Nigerian magistrate has written:[19]

> It is rare to find the wives in a polygamous home acting in unison all the time. There is always a rivalry among them as to who would be the husband's darling. In consequence each wife is often left to strive to give her children the best training she can, so that they may not be relegated in the future to a subordinate position among other children of the extended family. This situation which makes women fend for themselves and their children, has become not only part of Nigerian culture but of her Native Law and Custom. A woman who, being capable of making a living on her own, prefers not to work, is regarded as being indolent and the Native Court will not have much sympathy for her if she sues for a divorce.

Among the Creoles of Sierra Leone missionary influence has led to a great emphasis being placed on statutory monogamous marriage, but the great desire for large numbers of children on the part of the men leads to an extensive pattern of so-called 'outside wives'. The illegitimate children of these semi-official unions are readily accepted because of the status still associated with having a large number of children. As Harrell-Bond puts it:[20]

> Despite the trouble which may be occurring within the marriage as the result of the birth of an outside child, a man will be receiving congratulations from his friends and even from his relatives who usually welcome the new addition.

Her study reveals that it is not uncommon for a man to have as many as nine children born out of wedlock after marriage and it is not surprising that she found that arguments over extra-marital affairs were the greatest source of conflict within a marriage. (My son was rather bemused when invited by a Sierra Leonean friend to assist in a picnic for his children. They went round to ten different houses and collected eighteen children. The friend claimed fourteen as his own and the other four were cousins. He was not married.) The position of the outside wives may be insecure, but there is a certain status in being the mistress of a distinguished personality and, some girls will feel, 'it is better to be the mistress of the Honourable so-and-so than to be the wife of a carpenter'.[21] In a number of instances, the outside children will be brought up in the father's household with his legitimate children, but opinion among wives appears hotly divided on this issue. What is not in doubt is that in

Sierra Leone as elsewhere in West Africa a man will openly acknowledge the outside children, give them his name and accept responsibility for their upbringing.

### The position of women

Whether the home is harmonious or not, it is clear that the bonds between a mother and her children are very significant and endure right through adult life. In her struggle to give her children every opportunity, a woman will make endless sacrifices. The illiterate trader whose three sons were a lawyer, a doctor and a university lecturer is not at all unique. Because the wife inherits nothing directly from her husband, she has to strive for economic self-sufficiency, with the result that many women become very wealthy in their own right. The European who is filled with righteous indignation at the sight of a woman walking to market with a heavy load on her head whilst the man strides in front unencumbered, fails to realize that the woman is going to market to sell her goods and the proceeds will be her own; the man is frequently going simply to chat and drink with his friends. The number of independent business women, traders and contractors in West Africa must be far higher than in any European country. Women with no education at all may be trading on such a scale that they regularly fly to Europe on business. Girls begin to trade at a very early age, and again this can be misinterpreted as cruelty in the form of child labour. The smiling ten year old who sells me bananas in the evening after school would not see it in these terms: for her it is an indication of status and responsibility, and she takes pride in her trade.

Although men usually accept responsibility for the basic needs of their children, school fees are a heavy item to which the wife may also contribute. Even in a monogamous household a wife feels the need to prepare herself financially, not only to support her own children if the marriage should be in difficulties, but also in order that she can educate younger siblings as well as support her ageing parents when necessary. (The West African wife in Britain who insists that she herself must qualify, regardless of her husband's status, and must send substantial sums of money home on a regular basis, has to be understood in the light of these pressures.) As Titi Mabogunje points out:[22]

> It is against this background that one can appreciate why every woman in Nigeria strives to have a trade or profession. A Nigerian woman realizes that she shoulders the greater share of responsibility in bringing up the family than the man. She also realizes that her social status is determined by that of her husband. This is why many women slave away to pay for their

husband's higher education, either abroad or in Nigeria, before they worry about themselves. Native law and custom does not decree that a woman must maintain her husband or educate him, it however, attributes a man's fortunes after marriage to the good or ill luck which his wife has brought him. The ill health or ill fortune of a married woman is attributed to her poor upbringing or family heritage; that of her husband is blamed on her. She is accused of not exercising a good influence on him.

No one can fail to be impressed by the extraordinarily hardworking nature of African women. In many areas, they are the ones who grow the food for the family, and it is rare indeed to find women responsible solely for the care of their children and of the home, as is the case with many European women. Even domestic duties will be more demanding because of the nature of African hospitality. Custom puts women in a subordinate position to their husbands; they must flatter them and pay due respect at all times; women do not receive the superficial signs of respect that women in Europe used to expect. Men will normally be served food first, will walk ahead and so forth, except at European-type functions and official receptions when the European pattern is usually observed. (One Camerounian friend delighted in making a point, when holding a dinner party with Europeans present, of maintaining the 'custom of the village'. He always invited the men to come and be seated at the table first and to be served first with their food!)

These outward signs should not allow the real power and influence of women to be underestimated because economic independence is the real key. Within the framework of statutory law the position of women is similar to that in British law, but equality of pay has always been the norm. There may not be very many African women politicians, but it is commonly accepted that if the market women of Accra or Lagos want to overturn a politician he is in grave danger. Today women are found increasingly in all the highest walks of life as permanent secretaries and political commissioners, university professors, judges and so forth, and can combine these highly successful careers with the roles of wife and mother. In societies where children are so much valued, married women have not been penalized and pregnancy is accepted as normally associated with marriage. In Cameroun this is carried to its logical conclusion: mothers are not only given generous maternity leave, but on returning to work are allowed additional time off to breastfeed their babies.

Women, however, bear the main strains of changing attitudes. At a conference held at Ibadan on Women and Development it was made clear that educated West African women are dissatisfied with their role. In a paper which shows just how much educational opportunities had improved for women in Nigeria since 1947, when one woman graduated, to 1970 when 1,369 women students registered for degrees at Nigerian universities, a Nigerian professor, herself a married woman, conveys the ambivalent attitudes that exist: 'The educated Nigerian woman wants a friend and companion in her husband . . . but he interprets her demand for companionship as a curtailment of his freedom of movement and action.' She suggests that contemporary western education does not prepare a man to understand the obligations and restraints of the polygamous system, and that a young man today imagines that 'his grandfather had unfettered freedom and licence to take as many women as he liked and to treat them and discard them as he wished'. This can lead to many stresses for the young, educated wife, who as a result of her desire for a monogamous marriage, may be forced to accept illegal but stable alliances between her husband and other women. Her comments, and that of many others at this gathering of very successful professional women, indicate some of the tensions that exist, and a realization of what may have been lost by moving away from the restraints and security of the traditional system.[23]

### The children

One cannot begin to look at African society without being aware of the value placed on children. The significance of this, and of attitudes to children and to child-rearing, will be analysed by June Ellis in detail in the following chapter, but it may be useful to point out that children do not belong solely to their biological parents, and may not necessarily be brought up by them. As Helen Ware has pointed out:[24]

> that a child lives with his grandparent, an uncle, or even a distant cousin in no way implies that a family is breaking up. Unity is in fact maintained by dispersion. The basic family unit is a series of interlocking meshes rather than the isolated cell of western middle class norms.

The use of the term 'fostering' to describe the process by which children are brought up by those other than their biological parents is confusing because the word in English conveys a very different relationship. In West Africa, fostering is almost entirely with kin. It is seen as a normal part of the socialization process, and is one way family members help one another: a woman who is childless will beg a child from her more fortunate sister; a mother who is on her own will be sent a grandchild to keep her company; and a civil servant in the city will accept his brother's child as a member of the family so that he may benefit from better educational opportunities, but as Fiawoo has pointed out,[25] 'a common denominator of fostering is that the child should not sever genealogical ties with the lineage of its biological parents' and adoption as we know it is virtually non-existent in traditional society. Where statutory adoption laws have been introduced, as in Ghana, this has been initially at the request and for the benefit, of European residents who wish to adopt. It is essential for a social worker to appreciate that these terms are not used in the same way as they are in Britain and that there is usually no realization on the part of an African parent that adoption leads to a total severance of all ties. At the Ibadan seminar on the West African Child in Great Britain a Sierra Leonean social worker described how a mother had signed a consent to adoption form sent from England. When the social worker explained to her that this meant giving up all claims to the child permanently she was appalled and immediately asked for her daughter to come home.

A study carried out in Nigeria in 1973 showed that one-third of the adult Yoruba in the area, whether married or not, had at least one child living with them who was not their own.[26] Very often the family will decide the best place for a child even against the wishes of a parent. Harrell-Bond quotes a Sierra Leonean couple with six boys and one girl. It was decided to give the girl, then four and a half, to the wife's sister as she had no children of her own. The husband was accused of spoiling his daughter and, although he did not wish her to leave, reluctantly accepted the decision saying, 'But what could I do against all those women?' When the wife was asked how she thought the child would adjust to the change, she could not understand the implications of the question—after all 'my sister is the same as me'. Another wife described how she had been looking after her sister's child even before she was married and had just kept her and taken full responsibility for her until she was fifteen, without her real parents making any contribution.[27]

## Social life

One of the most enjoyable aspects of life in Africa is the open hospitality which forms the basis of social life, centred on the homes of friends and relatives. Formal invitations are the exception as friends visit each other spontaneously, and visitors, even strangers, will always be made welcome. If the family are at table, or about to eat, a guest will always be invited to join them. It is not usual to prepare food for a precise number of people, so the embarrassment of not having enough to go round does not arise. The guest may eat his fill if he is hungry or take a small amount as a token. Food is rarely wasted as there is always someone ready to consume the remains. The idea of having to postpone a meal until a visitor goes, or the embarrassment felt by many English people if a visitor arrives when they are eating, is hard for an African to understand. It is realized that white people do not welcome casual visitors and one of the most common complaints against European wives in Africa is that they are unwilling to provide food and drink at any time for anyone who may happen to call.

Equally, if one has been invited and is unable to attend this is not seen as an occasion for elaborate apologies and explanations. All these responses have to be learnt by the African in England, just as the British in Africa have to learn not to be surprised if their guest fails to turn up and at the next encounter offers no explanation. As one Nigerian lecturer put it: 'If I say I will go, it means I will go if I can. If I do not come they must know that a good reason has prevented me.' The hospitality of the home is all-important and it would be a near impossibility to refuse to entertain an unexpected visitor even if one had another engagement. If the latter is so pressing that it cannot be avoided, the African will usually handle it with charming courtesy, as on the occasion when we called on a friend who appeared elaborately dressed and obviously about to go out. We began to apologize and retreat, in the English manner, but he interrupted by saying that we had arrived at just the right moment to attend a reception for the Bishop who would be delighted to meet us. This left us entirely free to accept or reject the new invitation where no doubt we would have received a warm welcome. This lack of rigid time-keeping and precise long-term planning coupled with the inevitable uncertainties of life, leads to a relaxed attitude often misinterpreted by Europeans as sheer incompetence.

Greetings are usually very elaborate and the European, casual, 'good morning' appears downright rude to the Yoruba, who have a special greeting for every conceivable occasion. The complexity of these greetings must be quite bewildering to a Yoruba child brought up in Britain. In Cameroun, even if there are thirty people in a room, totally unknown to you, you will shake hands with each one in turn. When visiting his family with a returning student, I was formally introduced and shook hands with innumerable relatives, then speeches were made and libations poured, before informal conversation could begin. Such formality can in fact often make social relationships smoother than our very casual manners.

Elaborate greetings, prostrating, kneeling, embracing, are all common, but kissing is very rare, as is any intimate display of affection in public between men and women. Kissing on the lips is regarded as very unhygienic. I well remember the annoyed surprise shown by an English health visitor lecturing to a group of African social workers in London. She explained that eating food with the hands was a very unhygienic habit and was nonplussed when one of the social workers replied: 'not as bad as kissing—at least we wash our hands before we eat.' Buchi Emecheta describes a young Ibo girl arriving at Liverpool to join her student husband: 'Adah was stunned when he kissed her in public with everybody looking on. Oh my God, she thought, if her mother-in-law could see them she would go and make a sacrifice to Oboshi for forgiveness.'[28] Men holding hands, on the contrary, is a very common sight and has none of the connotations it would have in Britain. Often, as a gesture of friendship, the hand may be retained for some time after handshake. Embracing of members of either sex with whom one has strong bonds is very common, and this can be embarrassing to an English person if it occurs in a public place.

Physical contact and verbal communication are all-important but much less significance is given to written tokens of appreciation such as birthday cards. The idea of writing to children is also an alien one. Among the Yorubas, as among many other African people, one finds a code of behaviour designed to maintain smooth relationships between people, in which stories and proverbs are often used to convey unpleasant truths. In our society, which places a very high value on the plain truth, 'even if it hurts', the African desire to keep a situation pleasant and save face all round, is frequently misinterpreted as deceitfulness and lies. The man who wishes to leave an employer for a better job will explain that he has to take two weeks off to attend a funeral. It would be discourteous to say that he is made to work too hard or that the pay is not enough. In the same way, the parents who take their child away from a foster mother saying that an aunt has arrived from home and is going to care for the child, when in fact they have found a foster home which they prefer, may be attempting to resolve a dilemma in a tactful fashion. Social workers often feel frustrated by what they see only as a deliberate lie.

Social life is mainly spent with members of the same sex; husbands and wives do not usually go out together except when attending European-type functions. Men will drink together, and girls seen drinking in hotel bars can often be assumed to be prostitutes. Women spend a great deal of time in active visiting—their social life may revolve round the market or round each others' homes. West Africans travel vast distances to visit relatives and to participate in traditional ceremonies and family functions. The fact that so many people, particularly women and young children, seem to be constantly on the move is one of the most striking impressions when travelling about Africa. One of the reasons European wives may feel very isolated is because they have no network of women friends and relatives to form the basis of their social life and a husband, once he is back home in Africa, may tend to fall back into social life with his men friends. (I have witnessed a Nigerian husband explaining patiently to his English wife that, although he had been asked out, it was not 'expected' that she would attend. She asked whether she had been specifically requested not to attend, and found it difficult to accept what was quite obvious in the context.)

Holidays are regarded as occasions for visiting the family or friends; the idea of going to the sea or to the countryside would be very strange, but important religious celebrations as well as weddings and funerals will be occasions for the conspicuous display of clothes and the entertainment will be lavish. Of all peoples, the Yoruba are renowned for their love of clothes and jewellery—a high proportion of their income goes on these items. It can be hard when a British foster mother of limited means, who has agreed to reduce her charges to a mother pleading poverty, is later faced with such a splendid wardrobe!

**Religion, traditional beliefs and superstitions**

Religion permeates West African life. Christianity and Islam co-exist without excluding the influence of the traditional gods and the ancestors. There are none of the symptoms of religious conflict which unfortunately seem the norm in other parts of the world; at many official ceremonies libations will be poured and the spirit of religious toleration is symbolized by the Yoruba Oba or King, who is head of all the religious institutions of his community, and who may worship at any of them. Africans find European lack of faith hard to understand and they are also amazed at our superstitions, having been taught by the missionaries that all such beliefs are backward and primitive.[29]

> In spite of the changes brought about in the attitude of the people towards many things by almost a century of Christianity and education, belief in magic is still pervasive . . . . those who do not think of having recourse to its aid still take it for granted and act implicitly, not only on the assumption that magic exists, but that it has an objective reality.

These words were written by a Nigerian in the 1930s, but they are still true today and, with an increasing belief in the value of traditional culture, are less likely to be denied.

The student working for his exams who spends money on special magic to help him succeed does not sit back and wait for results, but redoubles his efforts; the use of magic in such a situation has been likened to the taking of pep pills by European students!

The attitudes to magic are mentioned not because they are

dominant in the lives of educated Africans, but because in times of stress they may have an increased significance. If an African believes that his failure is the result of evil forces being called in against him, it is no use just laughing this off. I know of one Nigerian woman, holding down a highly paid and very responsible job, who had spent twelve years in England, many of them under conditions of great hardship. She was absolutely convinced that her husband's second wife had cast a spell to prevent her return, and it was only when her own family had a counteracting charm prepared, that she was able to move freely. She described this experience to me graphically by saying that she had been locked up, but woke one morning to find that she was released and free to move as she wished.

Illness is frequently seen as the result of ill wishes from a jealous rival, and serious illness in Britain, understood by the family here to have physical causes, may be totally misinterpreted back home, with requests for large sums of money to perform the necessary ceremonies to ensure recovery. One man whose wife was dying of cancer tried to insist, against the advice of the hospital, on sending her back home because he was certain that her family would blame him for her death. In this case the social worker was able to obtain a letter from the specialist concerned, explaining the nature of the illness, the fact that the husband had given his wife every care and that nothing further could be done. In spite of this the husband felt afraid to return and face his in-laws.

It is easy to ridicule such thinking, but it is becoming increasingly clear that many of the so-called 'medicine men' or traditional healers are able to heal psychiatric disorders more easily than their western-trained counterparts. Many a West African doctor will now freely refer a patient to the traditional healer if he believes the illness to be primarily psychosomatic. It seems evident that in cases of mental breakdown in Britain many patients will make a more satisfactory recovery back home, although clearly this is not inevitably so, as the case history of the Armah family shows (see appendix).

**Social change**

Modern urban living, and particularly European types of housing, can impose a life-style which may lead to isolation and relative loneliness, but the strength of traditional culture still seems to overcome these physical constraints. The traditional family compound was elastic and room could easily be found for visitors, but even in a modern Lagos flat, room must be found. I stayed with a couple who could be regarded as fairly typical of those returned from the UK, and who were fortunate enough to have found a four-room flat. Both were graduates holding responsible jobs, and their two children, who had been born in Britain, attended a nearby private school. The husband's younger sister was attending secondary school and lived as a member of the household, taking the younger children to school and helping in the house in her spare time. The wife's eighteen year old brother who had left the village to look for work, and a second brother attending school, were the other regular members of the household. During my stay, the husband's mother was also there, having come to receive treatment at the hospital, and the wife's mother and father came for five days on a visit. When additional visitors came, the children slept on mats on the floor. It would just not be possible to say in the English fashion, 'I am sorry we can't put you up—we haven't a spare room.' If your family comes, room will be found.

This family willingly accepted their responsibilities to younger siblings whilst also benefiting from the help received, but others may try to avoid such involvement. To what extent the extended family is breaking down and how far change is desirable are frequent topics of debate among West Africans, in the press, on the radio and television, at learned conferences and in private conversation. Opinions are as varied as the participants. There are couples who deliberately choose not to return to their home areas, or even prefer to live in another country, because they feel they can have greater control over their own lives. It is not, they say, that they are opting out of their contributions to the family, but they like to make their own decisions and distribute their income as they wish, without the family knowing exactly what they earn. They will feel a duty to educate younger siblings, and probably nephews and nieces, but they draw the line at more distant connections who may expect support.

Some say that the extended family saps initiative and encourages idleness, that it holds back the individual from realizing his potential and encourages parasites who live on their more fortunate relatives. Much the same arguments are heard in Britain when the Welfare State is discussed. Indeed, the extended family may be seen as the West African equivalent of the Welfare State: it protects the least capable and, in a society without old age pensions or unemployment pay, it provides for disaster. As Nwogugu explains:[30]

> The experience of the political crisis and civil war in Nigeria between 1967 and 1970, showed the importance of the extended family in our social structure. In the former Eastern Region, for instance, most of the displaced persons who returned from other parts of the country found a ready welcome among members of their extended family. In addition when returnees had lost the tools of their trade, the extended family played a significant role in helping them to find their feet. This was important because no government in Nigeria at that time had

the ready financial and technical resources to deal with a national disaster of such magnitude.

In Europe we would have solved the problem by creating refugee camps.

In countries where it is not yet possible to have equal educational opportunities for all, the investment in one member of the family can lead to development for many more. As women marry young, and until recently would expect to bear children throughout their reproductive life, the age range between siblings may be very considerable. It is not uncommon for a young man at university to have brothers and sisters just starting school and he will be expected to bear the heavy responsibility of their school fees as soon as he starts earning. Lloyd calculated in 1967 that many graduates earning £2,000 p.a. would be spending at least 25 per cent of their income on education of kin, not their own children. He estimated that among lower paid junior staff the percentage contribution was a good deal higher.[31]

It is not uncommon within one family to find a wide occupational range within the same generation; a subsistence farmer, a doctor and a mechanic may well be brothers who keep in close touch in spite of their different life styles. I know of one family where the youngest brother became a minister in the government. His education had been paid for by his illiterate senior brothers, one of whom was a domestic servant and the other a peasant farmer; this had led to scholarships in Britain and Canada. This man had a clear obligation to finance the education of at least some of his brothers' children. One striking feature of this situation is that even as a minister he would feel no embarrassment at driving up in his Mercedes and parking it outside the simple quarters for domestic servants where his brother lived.

One would expect that the gap between the standard of living of members of the élite and their relatives in the village would create great tensions but this is not so; Africans seem to have a marvellous adaptability which enables them to cope with rapid change. No man is ever ashamed of the simplicity of his parents' way of life; the more humble his background, the more proud he is of the efforts that have been made to help him to his present position. Parents accept that Western education leads to a different life style which they do not fully understand and children contribute to their parents' material comforts without trying to change their way of living. (One very sophisticated Camerounian once brought his old, illiterate mother to visit us. She was not at all happy inside a western-style house and did not wish to join a mixed party at table. However, she sat very happily in a basket chair on the veranda smoking her pipe and drinking her bottle of beer.) Visits to the family home will be regular although the frequency will obviously depend on distance and may be less than desired because of the necessary expenditure on gifts. The city family used to all modern comforts will adapt to the village despite its lack of amenities unless they have really lost their roots, although they may take their camp beds and boiled water with them! Many will hope to retire there themselves and, for that reason, as well as to help the people back home, may devote considerable sums of money to modernizing their village. A glance at any Nigerian newspaper will give an indication of the large number of appeals being made to 'townsmen' to raise funds for a water supply, or for electricity, a new school or a town hall. A man's status will be greatly enhanced by what he puts back into his own community. What no one can now assess is how close these ties will remain with the next generation, born in the cities and only visiting their grandparents two or three times a year.

**Conclusions**

Educated Africans are caught up in a turmoil of changing values and this puts them under severe pressures. Student families in Britain, however long they stay here, will have to re-adjust to their own society when they return, and some understanding of the challenges they will then face should assist those who are working with such families to have a more realistic and meaningful approach. 'It was so much easier for our parents', a Nigerian sociology graduate once said to me,

> they believed in the white man's values as superior and wanted to do anything that would help their children to acquire them. We have seen your society and we want to pick and choose—to benefit from some aspects whilst rejecting those we feel alien to our traditional culture. The result is that we have become very confused and contradictory in our own behaviour and even in bringing up our children.

The dilemma for West Africans lies in deciding how to maintain the traditional values and yet adapt to and benefit from the modern industrialized world, which is with us whether we want it or not. To conclude with another Nigerian view:[32]

> I think our strong family ties and the feeling of identity with the group are some of the best features that our society possesses. In adopting formal education to suit our needs, these ideas must be inculcated in the young. We must learn from the mistakes of the west. We do not need to have our young people reject us and create communes to teach community feeling of their own, in a world where they had never been taught to

identify with their family and to feel responsibility for their family.

## Notes

1 P. C. Lloyd, *Africa in Social Change,* Harmondsworth, Penguin Books, 1967, p. 126.

2 M. M. Green, 'Land Tenure in an Ibo village', quoted in E. I. Nwogugu, *Family Law in Nigeria,* Ibadan, Heinemann, 1974, p. xxi.

3 N. A. Fadipe, *Sociology of the Yoruba,* Ibadan University Press, 1970, p. 118.

4 Ibid., p. 119.

5 Ibid., p. 128.

6 European women are frequently embarrassed when children or even adults carry their handbag. This is again merely a mark of respect.

7 Fadipe, op. cit., p. 134.

8 Nwogugu, op. cit., gives a very straightforward explanation of both statutory and customary marriage procedures in Nigeria. Fadipe gives a very detailed description of Yoruba traditional marriage procedures. Many of the novels give a picture of such practices both as they were in traditional society and as they have been adapted.

9 Claire Robertson, 'Ga Women and Socio-Economic Change in Accra, Ghana', in N. G. Hafkin and E. G. Bay (eds), *Women in Africa, Studies in Social and Economic Change,* California, Stanford University Press, 1976.

10 Christine Oppong, *Marriage among a Matrilineal Elite,* Cambridge University Press, 1974.

11 P. Marris, *Family and Social Change in an African City,* Routledge & Kegan Paul, 1961. It is not only in matrilineal households that husbands and wives may spend much of their time apart. In his study of Yoruba households in Lagos Peter Marris reported that a quarter of the wives in his study were not living with their husbands. 'Even where there is no question of divorce, husbands and wives may not live together' (p. 51, and see especially chapters 4 and 5).

12 B. E. Harrell-Bond, *Modern Marriage in Sierra Leone,* The Hague, Mouton, 1975, p. 171.

13 Nwogugu, op. cit., p. 51.

14 Oppong, op. cit., p. 30.

15 Nwogugu, op. cit., p. 178.

16 Ibid., p. 181.

17 Harrell-Bond, op. cit., p. 247.

18 A number of papers presented to the national conference on Nigerian women and development, Ibadan, 1976, made this very clear. Harrell-Bond's study, op. cit., shows not only the very high value placed on monogamous marriage by students, but also the illusions they hold concerning European marriages.

19 Titi Mabogunje in a paper, 'The Legal Status of Women in Africa', presented at the seminar on the African child in Great Britain, Ibadan, 1975. Quoted in the report of the seminar, Commonwealth Students' Children Society, 1975, p. 10.

20 Harrell-Bond, op. cit., p. 141.

21 Ibid.; for a detailed discussion of the status of children born out of wedlock see chapter 6.

22 Mabogunje, op. cit., p. 11.

23 Professor F. A. Ogunsheye in an unpublished paper, 'Formal Education and the Status of Women in Nigeria', presented to the national conference on Nigerian women.

24 Helen Ware in a paper, 'The Changing African Family in West Africa', in the report of the seminar on the African child in Great Britain, p. 8.

25 D. K. Fiawoo, 'The Concept of Child-Fostering in Ghana', in ibid., p. 12.

26 Helen Ware, op. cit., p. 12.

27 Harrell-Bond, op. cit., pp. 120-1.

28 Buchi Emecheta, *Second-Class Citizen,* Allison & Busby, 1974, p.36.

29 Fadipe, op. cit., p. 292.

30 Nwogugu, op. cit., p. 332.

31 Lloyd, op. cit., p. 187.

32 Ogunsheye, op. cit.

Chapter Three

# The child in West African society

*June Ellis*

A mother's son is a buttress:
if you have none
down falls the house.
A mother's daughter is your
everyday apparel:
if you have none
you're cold, exposed.

(Ewe poem)

Although children are of great importance in West Africa and not to have children is probably the greatest single misfortune that can happen to anyone, West African society is not child-centred. Socialization proceeds on the assumption that the child is passive and simply has to learn to adapt to the requirements of society. Whereas in Britain there is increasing support for the idea that one should take account of the needs and pre-dispositions of individual children and try to help them realize their potentialities, this is a notion that is foreign to West Africa with its emphasis on the over-riding importance of the group. Appropriate child-training is axiomatic and the child is thought to grow up in a relatively unproblematic way. True, he may behave badly and require punishment and close surveillance but this occurs within an accepted framework, and parents or other agents of socialization do not question the very basis of their actions. This is in some contrast to Britain where child-training tends to be exacting and time-consuming and many parents wonder anxiously just what is in the best interests of their children.

Thus, there are significant differences between the two societies in the way they think about children. In Britain, attitudes are affected by psychological and especially psychoanalytic ideas.

Thus importance is attached to specific experiences at particular times, whose influence may linger on, and the early years are thought to be crucial. Traditional society, almost by definition, is one in which actions are not subject to critical analysis, and psychological theories, which take as their starting point the behaviour of the individual, are not likely to be very compelling even should they impinge on traditional thought. In my experience, West African university students have expressed outright incredulity when confronted with ideas about early critical periods in children's development that have gained wide acceptance in Britain. The West African does not think of the child in individual developmental terms but, instead, has a view of him as capable of adapting easily to new situations and readily putting behind him unpleasant experiences.

## The importance of children

It has been said of West Africa, 'To leave no heirs behind him is the worst evil that can befall a man,'[1] and the Tallensi go even further in maintaining that to die childless is to live in vain.[2] The crucial importance of procreation cannot be overstressed. Field, in an ethno-psychiatric study in Ashanti, points out that 'parenthood is more highly valued than marriage, even with educated girls'.[3] An anecdote provides further support for this. Two unmarried Salvation Army nursing sisters from Britain, who ran a maternity clinic in a rural area, recounted how their patients invariably asked them where their husbands were. The women were a little puzzled when the nurses said they had no husbands but the negative answer to the question 'But where are your children?' was one that baffled the African women utterly. They simply could not understand this childlessness and that the two should accept their childless state with such apparent equanimity.

Not only is there a great desire for children but there is a wish for *many* children and this is not limited to people in the rural areas and to those with little education. In Ghana, there are no signs of a lower fertility rate amongst the professional classes.[4] Lloyd comments on the Nigerian élite: 'The surprising feature of educated families is their large size. While educated women in other parts of the world have tended to limit the number of children they bear, elite families of four are modal . . . and completed families of six children are common in Ibadan.'[5] Confirmation of pregnancy is likely to be a time of jubilation even when a woman already has several children. We can perhaps draw a contrast with research findings in America: in a major study of attitudes to child-rearing it was found that only 62 per cent of the American women interviewed were delighted to be having a first child and they became less delighted at the prospect of subsequent children, only 34 per cent expressing such emotions at later pregnancies.[6]

Delight at having children must be linked with the fact that they are seen not as liabilities but as potential assets: 'The traditional West African view of children is an instrumental one. The stress is not on the child in his own right but children are seen very much in terms of their utility and the way they enhance the status of their parents.'[7] [8] The idea that one should have as many children as possible is not at all uncommon though it is tempered somewhat nowadays by a consideration of the economic strains of caring for children. It is possibly only in the rural areas, where however most people live, and where children's contribution to the family economy remains, that one will find people who, when asked about preferred size of family, answer 'the bigger the better'. One who does answer in this way, at least by implication, is an old Ghanaian, 'I feel I am the happiest man in the village for, at present, I have thirty children. You would like to see me with my three wives and thirty children around us in the evening telling Ananse[9] stories. Again, because of my children I scarcely work on the farm and, above all, I am highly respected in the village.'[10] (It was also said, in praise of a leading member of the new government in Ghana in 1966: 'A great man; twenty-two children already and two wives still worth producing.'[11])

## Childlessness

Where fertility is so important, to be childless is unenviable. 'Parents are generally worried when their daughters do not become pregnant within the first year of marriage.'[12] Fortes has written of Ashanti (and this comment would hold throughout West Africa): 'childlessness is felt by both men and women as the greatest of all personal tragedies and humiliations.'[13] The barren individual is not invited to comment on public affairs nor expected to do so. In a society where there is strict age-grading, and where to show 'disrespect' is the cardinal offence, even small children may taunt the childless.[14] Deviance tends to be attributed to wickedness; 'The fact that a couple have no children is regarded as a proof that they are bad people and they are being punished with childlessness by God.'[15] Or—and this is perhaps particularly felt by the childless themselves—the wickedness is seen as residing elsewhere, as resulting from the spite and evil wishes of others: for 'It is in relation to disorders of the reproductive system, whose efficient functioning is a matter of the greatest concern, that explanations involving witchcraft are most invoked.' [16] [17]

Since the procreation of children is of such compelling importance in traditional West African society, the question of deferring the start of a family or of refraining from having children whilst in Britain, may appear to West African students to be irrelevant or worse: the practical difficulties of caring for children in Britain paling into insignificance beside more basic feelings. And the comfort that may be gained from the link with the family in West Africa that children provide for students who are far from home, should not be discounted.

### The living and the dead

The birth-rate may be high but infant deaths are still distressingly common in tropical Africa and this partly explains the desire to have many children and, at the same time, itself demands an explanation. Traditional religion offers this. The belief in reincarnation makes possible a more accepting view of the wastage of young lives. Just as the ancestors are thought to have gone from the land of the living, though not far, the newborn are regarded as not fully and securely with the living and are thought to have special links with the spirit world. Throughout West Africa the stillborn child, and one who dies before he is named, is suspected of being a spirit child, 'one of those wicked children who, when they died, entered their mothers' wombs to be born again'[18] and is buried without ceremony and not mourned. In Yoruba society, these children are called 'abiku':[19]

> after living on earth for a short time, they leave to rejoin their spirit companions who have all the while been urging them to return. After one child has died in infancy or early life the next, of either sex, may be suspected of being 'abiku'. The parents scrutinize the baby's body for birthmarks and small physical peculiarities which it seems to share with its predecessor. If she suspects that this is the 'same' child, the mother takes the utmost pains to persuade it to stay, calling it pathetically by special names such as 'Malomo—Do not go again'; 'Banjoko—Sit down and stay with us'; and 'Duro oro iko—Wait and see how you will be petted' . . . . In any wayward behaviour the mother imagines the 'abiku' is threatening to leave her and she treats his every wish with excessive concern. When he runs out of sight at dusk she thinks he has gone to dance with his spiritual playmates beneath the baobab tree . . . .

### Welcoming the child

Happily, most children do not die and the safe delivery of a healthy infant is a cause for family rejoicing and there are special ceremonies and rites to be performed. In Ghana there is an 'outdooring' ceremony about seven or eight days after the birth. Early in the morning, the baby is brought outside for the first time and placed under the eaves or in the shade of a tree. His mother, who is thought in childbirth to have been 'between life and death' will be wearing the new clothes bought for the occasion by her husband. Family and friends come to offer their congratulations and to welcome the newcomer. Drinks are served, libations poured to the ancestors, and prayers, similar to the one below, offered. Such a prayer shows the concern with life that suffuses traditional West African religion (so often thought of by outsiders as preoccupied with darkness and death) and it also indicates societal values that will be important for the child; values such as respect and co-operation.

> May all we do prosper — Amen
> May we all come together when summoned — Amen
> May we find water when we dig a well — Amen
> And when we drink thereof may we feel satisfied — Amen
> May this child always look ahead — Amen
> May he respect his elders — Amen
> Long life to his father and mother — Amen
> And may he work to support us all — Amen
> May members of this lineage forgive his faults — Amen
> May he not steal, neither be wicked — Amen
> Ladies and gentlemen, are we agreed upon this? — Amen[20]

## Names

Words are very powerful in African culture: they are an essential part of all traditional medicine and in magic it is thought that a person can be harmed through using his name. The naming of a child not only marks his acceptance as a member of the society but it does more than this, as it is widely maintained that the giving of a name creates a person. Maclean observes: 'Naming is regarded as an important means of establishing the reality and power of both objects and individuals; thus the named baby is felt by all to have had its existence confirmed and strengthened.'[21] A child who dies before he is named will not be 'counted' by the parents as having lived (a factor which should not be overlooked in demographic studies!); on the other hand, a child who dies just after naming will always be remembered.

The names a child is given tend to place him in his family or society. For the Yoruba,[22]

> The numerous names that are given at this time link the newcomer with his dead ancestors and with the presiding gods.

> If the mother has implored a particular orisha (god) to grant her this child, she will acknowledge her gratitude in its name. If a grandfather has recently died, the name 'Babatunde', meaning 'father has returned', will clearly demonstrate the conviction that the ancestors live on in their descendants . . . .

Many names, such as the Ibo 'Nwabueze—Children are priceless' and 'Chinyere—God's gift', reflect the deep joy that children are felt to bring. In Ghana, it is often the case, also, that a child is called by his or her 'day' name. Thus, a boy born on a Friday is 'Kofi'. The naming of a first child marks a change in status of the parents who come to be known as, for instance, 'Kofi's mother' and 'Kofi's father' and, in traditional society, address one another in this way. Middle-class English mothers may express resentment at being referred to as 'Jane's mother' or 'Peter's mother' and insist that they are individuals in their own right and not 'just' someone's mother. Such a form of address is regarded as a badge of honour in West Africa.

**Care of the young baby**

Great attention is lavished on the new baby, who is everyone's favourite. Of course, in hardly any societies in the world are small infants treated harshly, but the extended family, with so many helping hands around, makes very indulgent care easily possible, and a baby is never left alone. Uka, who investigated child-training in three major Nigerian tribes: the Yoruba, the Ibo and the Ibibio writes,[23]

> In all areas studied, the child receives a great deal of love and warmth. He receives affection not only from the mother but also from relatives and friends of the family. He is carried whenever he cries. In the rural areas the mother shares her bed with the infant in her own hut . . . . If a child cries at night he is picked up immediately and fed or cuddled. If the cry persists, a bush lamp is lighted and the parents are forced to stay awake.

It may be that the 'separation anxiety' that children in Britain tend to show at around nine months when their mother leaves them, or someone else holds them, is not found in West Africa where babies are accustomed to being handled by a range of people. Certainly it is not nearly as common as in Britain and West Africans do not expect other people's children to react to them with fear.

Two further ways in which the treatment of young children in West Africa differs from practices in Britain should be pointed out because they can give rise to considerable misunderstandings. First, although the child experiences much more of the comfort that comes from continuous close bodily contact than a child in Britain, in West Africa there is little fondling and kissing of infants and any kind of caressing stops when the child is toddling. In Uka's Nigerian survey, 'Many parents spoke seriously against it [kissing].'[24] West Africans express their caring in a different way, through good physical attention, such as bathing, skin-care and hair-care, which are all very important in a tropical climate. They would be likely to regard the actions of British parents as mawkish and sentimental. Second, verbal behaviour is regarded differently. In Britain, mothers tend to talk to their infants from an early age but in West Africa the mother will talk to her child when he 'has sense' and is able to talk to her in return. A Yoruba colleague has made the observation that someone from her tribe would regard talking to a baby as about as sensible as addressing a stone. This difference in approach is brought out beautifully in the autobiography of an Ibo mother, Adah, who recounts her struggles to bring up her five small children alone in London. When she goes to pick up her children at the nursery:[25]

> Her baby was gurgling at nothing in the pram. She even gave a smile of recognition when she saw her mother. Adah did not have much time to talk to her as she was supposed to be doing. It took her a long time to learn this ritual of talking to a baby, who either did not understand or, in most cases, did not know what to make of it. In England they say it's very good to chatter to your child, even when it is a few hours old, so she too started doing it, but would make sure that none of her people were around. They might well think her a witch, talking to something that did not answer back.

## The beginning of childhood

But even if he is not hearing 'baby talk' or being kissed, the West African baby's life is a good one. His cosseted existence is brief, however, and ends with weaning or, at the latest, when he begins to walk and talk. Considerable variation in practice is reported for weaning. It can be attempted before a year, or left until very much later; be gradual or abrupt. The child may be persuaded to give up the breast by providing desirable alternatives, or he may simply lose interest as the breast milk begins to fail. Often, however, there appears to be an element of coercion. 'It is widely believed that the milk of a pregnant mother is harmful for a child and, for this reason, children may be weaned suddenly if the mother discovers that she has conceived again.'[26]

In her work on the Ga tribe, Field makes the point that the Ga mother appears to lose interest in her child once it ceases to be a baby, 'the mother usually seems to be interested in a child while it remains the youngest.'[27] This is probably an overstatement but, certainly, the child's world changes sharply about the time he is weaned. He is treated with some strictness and he must learn to respect and to obey those who are older than himself, and to revere old age.

## Family structure

Family structure is a most important factor in child-training. The experiences of a child in the restricted nuclear family of western industrialized society are very different from those of a child in the extended family of West Africa, and have different consequences. And despite growing urbanization, the extended family remains significant. Caldwell makes an interesting comment on the continuation of traditional patterns of residence in Ghana: 'Many more Ghanaians now live in large town houses containing a considerable number of rooms. In one sense, this has represented a surprisingly successful attempt to carry a village way of life into the town.' He adds that in Accra, where there has been a great deal of new building, more than half the population live in houses containing more than twenty people.[28] The West African child can be understood only within the context of this all-important social network. He is rapidly drawn into the total life of the group, learning to relate to many different people and acquiring a sensitivity to group approval and a sense of the overriding importance of kinship ties. These ties are further emphasized and strengthened by the practice of kinship fostering. This is widespread in West Africa and Pat Stapleton discusses it in Chapter two. Kinship fostering is to be distinguished from crisis fostering, which only occurs when parents are unable to care for the child. It is an important and recognized part of the normal socialization process and many West African children will spend long periods away from their own biological parents, but within the family.

## Authority and respect

Family life is more formal and ordered in West Africa than in Britain and, from the start, the child is made aware of seniority in his relationships with other children as well as adults. Fortes has observed of the Ashantis: 'an older sibling is entitled to punish and reprimand a younger brother or sister and must be treated with deference'[29] and, among the Tallensi, 'from the authority of parent over child is derived that of elder sibling over younger. It is equally absolute'.[30] At meals, the oldest child will supervise the sharing of the food (children will not normally eat with adults) and has the right to the first and largest helping. 'It is the duty of the youngest child to wash up the bowl when the meal is finished.'[31]

If the system into which the child is integrated is based on seniority, it is regulated by notions of respect. This idea of respect permeates the whole of traditional society and it is probably very difficult for any European to grasp fully its meaning and significance. 'Being disrespectful' when said of a child in Britain, may mean he is being slightly pert and such behaviour may even, upon occasion, be admired. In West Africa, the sharpest reproof of all is 'this child is disrespectful to elders'.[32] 'From a very early age, Nigerian children are taught to cultivate respect for parents and other members of the family. The child must show respect to all who are older than he. In Yorubaland, children are expected to prostrate or genuflect when greeting elderly people.'[33] 'The essence of customary education of the Ewes of Ghana', writes Nukunya, is 'the learning of "amembubu", which means respect for all who are senior to the child in age, and from an early age the child is taught the correct forms of address.'[34] Azu paints a very similar picture in relation to the Gas: 'From about five years onwards the women step in to teach the child what language is to be used when talking to older people.' 'One often hears this admonition . . . "one does not talk to an elder in this manner."' And correction continues, 'There are moments when even youths are corrected, especially when they are talking to elders. To make a person conscious of what he says, fines may be levied on him for any unguarded speech.'[35]

Kaye, in discussing children's speech, begins his chapter with this very revealing quotation: 'A good child is the one who does not say anything until he is told to do so.' He goes on,[36]

> It is generally considered a sign of disrespect for a child to address an adult, except in reply to a question. Children are expected to lower their voices politely when replying to adults' questions. In the presence of visitors, children are required to sit quietly without saying anything, or to leave the room. . . . A child who reminds an adult he has forgotten something is scolded. . . .

It seems universally the case that children are told never to interrupt grown-ups. Uka, in his study of three Nigerian tribes, reports: 'When parents converse with other adults, children are not expected to listen in. If they are present, they must only be seen and not heard.'[37] This is clearly a long way from a society where a three year old can say 'silly daddy' and only call forth mild amusement!

Respect is more than obedience and it includes the idea of

honour, but obedience is an important part of respect and is to be justified in the same kind of terms. Some comments from a survey of Ga adolescents[38] are interesting here: 'Our fathers are like Gods and our mothers also. . . . We in no reason have to challenge them even if your opinion is the right one.' The respondents frequently referred to the 'bringing forth' of children as a justification for unquestioning obedience on the part of these children: 'Because they born you, so they can do to you whatever they think is right.' Of the 350 children questioned, the overwhelming majority took the view that it was absolutely wrong to disobey parents or call into question their actions and, although one must recognize that they are speaking in 'ideal' terms, and that what actually happens might be somewhat different, it can be said that these comments represent a view of parent-child relationships that is strikingly different from that in Britain.

The strictness of traditional upbringing has already been mentioned and it is generally accepted that punishment is a very important part of caring and a necessary part of good parenthood. It is interesting that a substantial number of these same Ga adolescents when asked what they *liked* about their parents, specifically mentioned punishment: 'my father punishes me to be good'; 'she insults me . . . when I am bad.' When they were asked how they thought they would train their own children, most respondents—and they themselves appeared to be being brought up strictly—said that they would favour even greater strictness. The kind of reasons they advanced for their views were, 'Because I want my child to be more respectful than I am. I want my child to work harder than I do and help me more than I help my parents.' These views turn on the idea that a person is not 'naturally' good and that, to help him to be good, severity of training is necessary: 'If a person is trained strictly, then that person becomes a good person'; 'If you would not train them strictly, he or she would be a bad girl or boy.'[39] These comments capture the essence of traditional thinking about human nature, which is somewhat pessimistic and which underlies a good deal of practice. Further it is believed that adversity is no bad thing.

## Socialization techniques

In view of the attitudes discussed above, and taking account of the lack of emphasis on individuality in traditional society, it is not surprising to find that the emphasis in socialization tends to be on negative sanctions rather than positive reinforcement. Indeed, it appears to be thought that virtue should be its own reward. Among the Ijaw, for instance, 'Some mothers state they do nothing to reward their sons or daughters because . . . not scolding them should be reward enough.' They believe direct praise turns the head of the child, causing him to become proud and to refuse to work. To say 'thank you' adults claim is sufficient. Children agree by saying they expect nothing from their parents for proper behaviour.[40]

Much the commonest punishment is 'beating' and it is widely held that to 'spare the rod is to spoil the child'. The use of the term 'beating' in West Africa does not, however, carry the same meaning as in Britain, and is certainly not to be equated with battering. It is more general in application than in Britain, where it would usually refer to a hard and prolonged dose of physical punishment. It *could* mean this (and often a stick is used) but it could also refer to 'smacking' or 'slapping'. A child may be beaten by his mother or father, by older siblings and, in theory, by other members of the family. In practice, the beating of children, for instance, by another of the father's wives, may cause great trouble. What should be noted is that these punishments are likely to be meted out in a fairly public situation and, though they may be painful, they are unlikely to get out of hand and go beyond what is culturally acceptable. Not only are there plenty of people around to see what is happening and to prevent punishment going too far, but parents are unlikely to reach the level of exasperation of parents in Britain. They are not committed to child-training techniques that require great reserves of parental patience and forbearance, and bonds of affection are not so narrowly focused. Children can, and do, go to others, not only for love and attention, but also for protection, if they think they are being unjustly punished.

Another common approach with offending children is to 'abuse' them verbally. They are upbraided and 'insulted' in no uncertain terms. Since both beating and verbal abuse are carried out where others can see and hear what is going on and 'others' would include peers and even those younger than the offending child, they carry with them the additional element of shaming. In the study of Ga adolescents already referred to, [41] it is clear that they felt very keenly being 'disgraced' in front of others. As might be expected, in a society where the group is so important, there is deliberate use of shaming as a technique of control. For instance, from many different sources there come accounts of the use of shaming in the treatment of bedwetters.

The inculcation of fear is another part of traditional methods of control and is to be viewed in the non-psychological context of traditional life, which is itself suffused with a sense of the strange, the inexplicable and the fearful. Uka remarks: 'Nigerian mothers use fear as a disciplinary measure, and reports from mothers say that it works well especially with young children.'[42] It may be used to get a child to stop crying or to go to sleep: 'advantage is taken of the fearful shrieks and cries of nocturnal birds and animals, such as owls, bats and monkeys',[43] or children may be threatened that a white man will come and get them if they behave badly!

### The child in society

As well as caring for younger brothers and sisters, children in West Africa contribute in many ways to the life of the group and are able to recognize themselves as useful members of it. Uchendu writes of an Ibo village:[44]

> Children take an active and important part in the work of the compound and the village. Mat making and carrying mud for house building are services which children are expected to render to any villager. Food is the only reward for such communal work. Children fetch firewood and carry water in large gourds or clay pots skilfully balanced on their heads.

Kaye records that,[45]

> In most Ghanaian homes, children are expected to take part in the work of the house from a very early age, and they may have simple household duties allotted to them from the age of three or even two. At this age they may follow their mothers, and help to bring in firewood. By the time they are five or six, most children have a program of chores for which they are responsible.

There is something to be said for a society where a child can have a meaningful role, like this, and to wonder whether in Britain too little is expected of children, their activities being restricted almost entirely to play.

The economic integration of West African children is paralleled by their involvement in adult social life. They are part of the 'real' world in a way that British children are not, and they are not regarded as 'in the way'—perhaps because of the self-effacing way they have been taught to behave. Green, in describing the Ibo, writes of 'a general participation of young and old in most matters of public concern'[46] and Uchendu, referring to Ibo children from a different region, comments: 'They are literally everywhere. They are taken to the market, to the family or village tribunal, to funerals, to a feast, to the farm and to religious ceremonies . . . . If there is a social or ritual ceremony going on in an Ibo village everybody is welcome.'[47] And of Ghana it is said: 'The evening is the time for telling stories, and adults and children gather round the fire to listen to traditional folk tales . . . .'[48]

## Children's play

Children also have many opportunities for play and enjoyment with their own companions. Camara Laye's book *The African Child* is a vivid account of a traditional childhood in Guinea, full of simple pleasures and revealing a closeness to nature that we, perhaps, have lost.[49] In West Africa, the sun is almost always shining and in the traditional village or compound there is plenty to do: mud, and sticks and stones to play with. Children are inventive, making cars and lorries from biscuit tins and cotton reels, although they are likely to have little opportunity to play with the kind of 'educational' toys, involving manipulative and motor skills, that are commonly found in Britain.

There is little attempt, such as we have in Britain (certainly in middle-class Britain) to create a child's world. Of course, the creation of such a world implies that the adults take the child as a starting-point and, in a society where age is venerated and individuality unstressed, this is not likely to occur. The close interaction with children *at their level* that constructive play requires, is not appealing in the African traditional world; it may not even be comprehensible. As one child said to me: 'I do not play with my parents; I respect them.' And a mature Ghanaian student with a growing family, explained in a psychology seminar that, as much as he would like to play with his children—he believed such play was emotionally and intellectually important for them—he could not for fear of what his own parents would say. Failure to take into account children's play needs may not matter too much in a traditional setting; there are plenty of natural play materials at hand and, since most activities take place out of doors, the child is part of a rich, ever-changing stimulating environment. Life could be very different in a small flat in Britain and failure to provide things for a child to do, and toys for him to play with, may matter very much more.

It may be readily deduced that the West African approach to formal schooling is 'traditional' also, using the word in the sense it might be used in England when referring to education. There is a great concern with achievement and standards, but little in the way of 'guided discovery methods' or 'child-centred' education. The average child at infant and junior school level in West Africa is likely to be in advance of a child in a British school, in formal and rote attainments. Education is taken very seriously there. This emphasis on earnest application may be illustrated by the comments of a Nigerian nursery school teacher on a four year old child. She said he was not working hard enough and that, if he did not make greater efforts, he would not be successful in the future. It is generally believed that hard work will ensure success. Little account is taken of differences in individual capacity and this bears hard on those children of modest ability who carry their family's expectations.

**West Africa and Britain**

There are then fundamental differences in the approach to the child in West Africa and Britain, and it is important not to minimize these. In West Africa, the child experiences quite a different social reality from that of the British child: different concepts of the good child and the good parent lead to correspondingly different expectations for behaviour.[50]

In West Africa, a parent who consulted with a child, and took into account the child's views in matters concerned with his welfare, would be regarded as failing in parental duty: 'But he is just a child', they would say, implying that he could not know what was good for him; a child who was lively and questioning, and whose curiosity would be likely to meet with approval in Britain would, in West Africa, be viewed as disrespectful. It follows, too, that where the group is of prime importance, as in West Africa, qualities like self-reliance and independence, will not be stressed in child-training. It has been said: 'Unity is strength . . . one who does not move with others is a bad person.'[51] It is not that in West Africa the child does not 'express himself' but that he expresses himself in a different way, as a group member and in relation to others.

Though there are losses in personal freedom, there are gains in the security that comes from being an integral part of a vast, supportive network in which family members are interchangeable, in a way they are not here, and will readily assume responsibility for one another's interests. The British child who, for some reason has to leave his mother and be cared for by a more distant relative, suffers an undeniable loss; the West African child who is sent to stay with a relative is deepening his experience of the family. The child's security is much less precarious than in Britain, where it is finely balanced in relation to one or two individuals. It must be admitted also that the introduction of a psychological dimension, which leads to a greater consideration of a child's feelings, is not without disadvantages. In Britain, it has contributed to an uncertainty about parental role and, in so far as this uncertainty communicates itself to the children or results in inconsistent parental handling, it is to be deplored. Against this, it can be seen that the time-honoured and non-reflective approach of the West African parent has a great deal to offer in providing an ordered and predictable set of experiences for the child.

## Notes

1 J. Jahn, *Muntu,* Faber & Faber, 1961, p. 109.

2 M. Fortes, *The Web of Kinship among the Tallensi,* Oxford University Press, 1949, pp. 168-9.

3 M. J. Field, *Search for Security,* Faber & Faber, 1960, p. 28.

4 J. C. Caldwell, 'Population Prospects and Policy', in W. Birmingham *et al.* (eds), *A Study of Contemporary Ghana,* Allen & Unwin, 1967, p. 153.

5 B. B. Lloyd, 'Education and Family Life in the Development of Class Identification among the Yoruba', in P. C. Lloyd (ed.) *The New Elites of Tropical Africa,* Oxford University Press, 1966, p. 166.

6 R. Sears, E. Maccoby and H. Levin, *Patterns of Child-Rearing,* Evanston, Illinois, Row, Peterson, 1957, p. 36.

7 D. Jibowu, 'Concepts of Motherhood', report of a seminar on the African child in Britain, Commonwealth Students' Children Society, 1975, p. 11.

8 B. Kaye, *Bringing up Children in Ghana,* London, Allen & Unwin, 1962, pp. 22-39.

9 Ananse is a spider man who is the hero of Ashanti folk tales. Collections of Ananse stories are listed in the bibliography.

10 Kaye, op. cit., p. 27.

11 G. Bing, *Reap the Whirlwind,* MacGibbon & Kee, 1968, p. 405.

12 N. Uka, *Growing up in Nigerian Culture,* Ibadan University Press, 1966, p. 30.

13 M. Fortes, 'Kinship and Marriage among the Ashanti', in A. R. Radcliffe-Brown and D. Forde (eds), *African Systems of Kinship and Marriage,* Oxford University Press, 1950, p. 262.

14 Kaye, op. cit., p. 27.

15 Ibid., p. 29.

16 U. Maclean, *Magical Medicine: A Nigerian Case-Study,* Allen Lane, The Penguin Press, 1971, p. 41.

17 F. Nwapa, *Efuru,* Heinemann, 1966. This Nigerian novel tells the story of a woman who thinks she is barren, of the way she suffers and of the remedies sought from a traditional healer. Her mother rejoices when she hears Efuru is pregnant at last, saying, 'My enemies will no longer rejoice.' But Efuru is bewitched, she cannot know the joys of motherhood, and her only child dies.

18 Maclean, op. cit., p. 51.

19 Ibid., p. 51.

20 G. Azu, *The Ga Family and Social Change,* Leiden, Afrika-Studiecentrum; Cambridge, African Studies Centre, 1973, Appendix ii, pp. 122-3.

21 Maclean, op. cit., p. 56.

22 Ibid., p. 56.

23 Uka, op. cit., p. 34.

24 Ibid., p. 76.

25 B. Emecheta, *In the Ditch,* Barrie & Jenkins, 1972, p. 11.

26 Kaye, op. cit., p. 70.

27 M. J. Field, *Social Organization of the Ga People,* Crown Agents for the Colonies, 1940, p. 31.

28 J. C. Caldwell, 'Population: General Characteristics', in W. Birmingham, ed., op. cit., p. 67.

29 Fortes, op. cit., p. 273.

30 Ibid., p. 35.

31 Kay, op. cit., p. 85.

32 G. K. Nukunya, *Kinship and Marriage among the Anlo Ewe,* Athlone Press, 1969, p. 32.

33 Uka, op. cit., p. 78.

34 Nukunya, op. cit., p. 32.

35 Azu, op. cit., p. 41.

36 Kaye, op. cit., pp. 166 and 170.

37 Uka, op. cit., p. 78.

38 J. Ellis, 'Child-Training in Ghana, with Particular Reference to the Ga Tribe', MA thesis, University of Ghana, 1968, p. 129.

39 Ibid., pp. 156-7.

40 P. E. Leis, *Enculturation and Socialization in an Ijaw Village,* New York, Holt, Rinehart & Winston, 1972, p. 59.

41 Ellis, op. cit., p. 89. For instance, of a father, it was complained, 'He insults me in front of my little sisters' and of a mother, 'If I do anything wrong she will stand in the house and speak so that everybody passing by will hear it.'

42 Uka, op. cit., p. 72.

43 Kaye, op. cit., p. 111.

44 V. C. Uchendu, *The Ibo of Southeast Nigeria,* New York, Holt, Rinehart & Winston, 1965, p. 62.

45 Kaye, op. cit., p. 194.

46 M. Green, *Ibo Village Affairs,* Cass, 1964, p. 79.

47 Uchendu, op. cit., p. 61.

48 Kaye, op. cit., p. 192.

49 Camera Laye, *The African Child,* Fontana/Collins, 1959.

50 For a further discussion of these issues see J. Ellis, 'Differing Conceptions of a Child's Needs: Some Implications for Social Work with West African Children and their Parents', *British Journal of Social Work,* vol. 7, no. 2, 1977.

51 A remark made by a Ghanaian schoolgirl.

Chapter Four

# Living in Britain

*Pat Stapleton*

> My dear young lady, in Lagos . . . . you may be living like an élite, but the day you land in England you are a second-class citizen.
>
> (Buchi Emecheta)

'Seeking the golden fleece' is how many West Africans describe the deep-seated ambition to travel to England for further studies; nourished by so much hope, their actual experiences, if they do succeed in reaching this country, are often so far from their dreams. Up until the 1950s, the number of students from Africa who managed to come to Britain was very small. They were, in the main, a group of hand-picked scholarship holders, many of them senior civil servants coming for some additional training prior to independence, medical students, lawyers called to the bar, and children of the very wealthy who may also have attended boarding schools in England, with only a sprinkling of the ambitious self-financed who feature so largely today.

Almost always these students came alone, leaving their wives and children behind, and so the problems of combining study and family responsibilities did not arise. The men travelling alone, of course, had other problems, particularly when they returned home and found that their wives did not understand their new ways of thinking and were often regarded as inadequate for the man's new western life style. This period marks the beginning of a number of mixed marriages, and at that time no doubt a white wife provided a certain status; however fear of him marrying a foreigner was one of the factors that led parents to encourage their sons to marry before leaving to go abroad, whether or not their wives accompanied them. These 'beentos'[1] as they were nicknamed, were highly regarded, and many of them on their return emulated things British, however inappropriate they might be in the home context. In those days a man would wear his heavy English suit in the hot sun so that everyone would know his status; today he is more likely to wear African clothes in Britain.

It was the obvious success of these students that encouraged so many others to follow in their path. Most of these old-timers look back on their experiences in Britain with happy memories, no doubt mellowed by time, but also reflecting the relatively privileged way they were treated. At that time there were very few black immigrants, and a black man was usually identified as a student even if taking on some manual work during vacations. The British Council and a wide range of societies involved the students in some aspects of British social life and politics. Students as a whole, of course, had a higher standing than they have today.

Since then the picture has changed dramatically. It is not possible to state with any accuracy the number of West African students now studying in Britain, and even more difficult to estimate the number of those who have wives and children in this country. British Council statistics for 1975/6 show a total of 7,500 from Nigeria, Ghana, Sierra Leone and the Gambia, registered as full-time students.[2] This figure does not include any of the many thousands of part-time students nor does it include anyone who has been in this country long enough to qualify for an LEA award. A study undertaken in 1972 of the position of West Africans in four London boroughs showed that over 75 per cent of the sample had been in Britain for more than six years and 40 per cent for more than eight years. It is not surprising that 85 per cent of the sample had children in this country.[3] None of these long-stay students will appear in any record as overseas students, although the many thousands who work and study part-time see themselves as temporary residents who intend to return home, and they deeply resent any attempt to identify them as immigrants; they are often supportive of tougher immigration restrictions, no doubt because they feel that the influx of West Indians and Asians has exacerbated feelings of racial prejudice and this rebounds on them.

## The students

We tend to think of students as young people on grants, financed adequately, if not generously, at the taxpayer's expense. The majority of West Africans do not come into this category at all. There are of course a number of government scholars, British Council scholars and other holders of special awards from the Commonwealth or the UN, but they are the minority. Although they may have problems, particularly if their scholarships are not really adequate, or are stretched to support a family, they form a comparatively privileged group. It is the vast number of private students, financed out of their own or their families' savings who face the most severe difficulties. Many of them are mature people, already married and with children, and they are frequently dependent on the ability of the wife to make a substantial contribution to the family income, and they face the most severe difficulties. A study sponsored by the United Kingdom Council for Overseas Student Affairs in 1971 showed that in a sample of sixty-one Nigerian students none was under twenty-five, and forty-one were over thirty; half the sample had come to Britain in 1963 or earlier.[4] It is the families of these long-stay students that are usually experiencing the widest range of problems, and are most likely to be in contact with social workers.

In spite of the growing number of universities in West Africa[5] the demand for places far exceeds the number available, and there is still a very serious lack of provision at the technical level. Coming to Britain therefore has provided and, in spite of increases in fees for overseas students, seems likely to continue to provide an answer, whether at the level of a PhD or at City and Guilds level. It is far easier to obtain a place at one of our polytechnics than at one of the West African universities which can be seen as the equivalent of Oxbridge. The enthusiasm with which overseas students have been recruited to Britain in the past, particularly by colleges starting new courses and needing to build up numbers, raises some fundamental questions. Does the college have any responsibility for the student once he has been accepted? Should it consider whether the course he is embarking on is appropriate? Should it have an obligation to provide adequate accommodation?

The major difficulties that students face are so interwoven that it is not easy to examine each one separately. They can be summarized under the headings of education, finance, accommodation, racial discrimination, care of children and marriage.

## Education

Many West African students do extremely well in Britain but others may start on the wrong footing because they have received very little guidance, if any, in seeking an appropriate course. They may attend a well-advertised private college whose qualifications will not be recognized or they may be registered for a course where the training is irrelevant to the needs of their own society. A student specializing in building techniques in cold climates and doing his practical work with a double glazing firm, is an extreme example. Some may have studied for years at home, by correspondence course, and after repeated attempts, obtained the necessary GCE 'A' levels to gain university entry, but be quite unable to follow a degree course. Their own educational background will almost certainly have placed a great deal of emphasis on learning by rote and their studies will have been carefully directed so that the more independent approach they will find in Britain can be very confusing. A student may have the capacity for higher studies, but be so unused to hearing English, as spoken by a wide variety of college lecturers in Britain, that he is completely at a loss when he first starts his course and may virtually lose his first term's work. Because of the way they have been taught, the majority of students are very slow readers. Faced with a long reading list at the beginning of term, and untrained in the art of selective reading, they may try and work through such a list, staying up to all hours and becoming so exhausted that they lose the power to concentrate at all. Sometimes time is lost in the first term due to late arrival, often as the result of immigration problems, so that the introductory period is missed and the student is without guidance. Many colleges now send out comprehensive information in advance, but if this reaches the student at all, it may only arrive as he is leaving, and will be read first of all on the plane.

These educational problems alone can cause failure, but coupled with a cold and unfriendly climate, lack of adequate funds, housing problems, worry over the children and the shock of colour prejudice, what is surprising is not that some take so long to succeed, but that so many make the grade at all.

Educational failure ties a student to Britain as shame will prevent him from returning home even if his family are urging him to do so. Elderly parents, who may not have seen their children for ten years or more, and are truly afraid of dying before they return, would prefer to see a son or daughter without a qualification than not see them at all. But to the failed student the anonymity of Britain may seem a better place than home where he will find his juniors better qualified. He knows how his return is anticipated for as Lloyd points out:[6]

> It is a rare parent who is not inordinately proud of his successful children. It is he who arranges the motorcade for the graduate returning from overseas, the church service of thanksgiving, and who demands that his son should wear his English winter suit as a public demonstration of his success. Achievements not available to the parents are realized in their children and their prestige and status in their own community are enhanced thereby.

Once having glossed over the real situation a student can quickly become caught up in a web of lies, so that even a wife may not realize that her husband is just going to the public library and reading newspapers all day, and not attending lectures at all. The case history of the Babalola family illustrates the near-impossibility of returning home once a false picture of success has been created. These failed students are so often older men for whom the disgrace seems the most acute.

Educational advice that can encourage a student to face reality, and channel his energies to an appropriate course, needs to be given by advisers with great sensitivity and awareness of the issues at stake. Clearly, it would be disastrous for a student to return without a qualification of any kind, so the essential help may involve gauging potential and assisting a student to achieve a more limited objective, rather than trying to persuade him to give up altogether. This applies as much to the women as to the men, as they tend to attempt a whole range of activities and will switch from dressmaking to computer courses and back again to cookery as the attractions of a particular course appear to suit their particular situation and working hours.[7] What must be remembered is that non-academic practical courses may permit a great earning potential for women in societies where there are an infinite number of small, private businesses.

## Finance

Financial worries are the root cause of many of the problems a student faces.[8] An adequate income would relieve him from worries about accommodation, would diminish the pressure on his wife to go out to work and would thus lessen the demand for day care and foster care. If wives were without economic pressures they could probably combine satisfactory arrangements for the care of the children with their own studies, which is not possible if they are combining study with several part-time jobs. Even when students are on grants, it is frequently found that these do not keep up with inflation. Grants are often not paid on time and so students may still have anxious months with no money coming in, unless they can earn it. Private students are, of course, the most vulnerable. All kinds of unforeseen events at home can cut off income. A sponsor may die and leave a student with no support at all, or funds can be reduced to a trickle because of problems of exchange control. The Nigerian civil war was an extreme case where many students were completely cut off from home, and those on government scholarships who refused to take an oath of loyalty to Nigeria not surprisingly lost their grants. Political changes can lead to the cutting off of funds and in all these cases the student has to fall back on his own resources. Students are no longer allowed to work without applying for work permits and many employers feel it is not worth the trouble to wait while this is obtained. Alternatively, unscrupulous employers will pay very low wages because they know the individual can have no legal redress. In any case, in times of economic crisis, it is always difficult for students of any nationality to get jobs and the sort of vacation earnings they could at one time rely on virtually disappear.

## Accommodation

Since universities in Africa are élitist institutions set in beautiful grounds with fine modern buildings, West African students naturally assume that in a 'developed' country like Britain conditions must be at least as good if not better. The reality of some of our colleges with their overcrowded and often old fashioned buildings scattered over a wide area, and with no residential accommodation, comes as a shock. Almost all educational provision in Africa, from secondary level upwards, has boarding accommodation, so there is an automatic assumption that this will be available. In fact, the biggest single problem that married students face is that of finding somewhere to live.

Although most colleges have welfare officers who do what they can in an impossible situation, very few, particularly in the London area, are able to recommend adequate accommodation at a reasonable rent for a man who arrives with his family or even with just his wife. Some families will be fortunate enough to obtain accommodation from a housing association or from one of the hostels that provide a limited number of family flats. They will be the lucky few. The majority of West African student families eventually find themselves in overcrowded multi-occupied houses with shared facilities—often cooking on an open landing and with an outside lavatory in the back yard to serve the whole house. Many are living in one room, with scarcely space to move between the double bed, which also serves as seating, and the table used for study and for eating. An oil stove is often used in an attempt to keep warm as cheaply as possible, and the children may be obliged to sleep on camp beds put down at night on the available floor space. Others may have more room but are often in a condemned property, faced with peeling wallpaper, damp walls, falling plaster, rats and other hazards.[9] Of course, they can go to the local authority and the health inspector will demand immediate action, but many families are illegal tenants with no rent books and they are very vulnerable to pressure from landlords. Constant harassment is one of the reasons leading to a decision to foster; it can take many forms: stealing mail, locking doors and frightening children. I have known six year old twins terrified to use the lavatory because it meant walking along a communal passage shared with the landlord who might jump out and shout at them. Even if the landlord is a fellow African the situation may be no better. He may be paying off a heavy mortgage and taking the maximum possible rent, benefiting from the prejudice which forces the tenants to his home, and it is not too surprising if he exploits others as he has been exploited.

Even if the family stay here long enough and qualify for local authority housing, the chances are that they will find themselves on an estate surrounded by those regarded as 'problem families'. Those authorities who feel it is best to put their problems together in the poorest and oldest housing, tend to include blacks among the 'problem' category. On some housing estates there is the curious situation where black families, who identify themselves with the middle class, being potential lawyers or accountants, do not allow their children to play outside with the rough white children from whom they will pick up bad language and bad habits. The white families on the other hand, may feel bitter at finding themselves with black neighbours making them even more clearly identified as belonging to a 'problem' group.

### *The new arrival*

On first arrival in this country, many students will stay with a friend. There is an automatic assumption that if your relative or fellow townsman is in Britain he will be ready to accommodate you, until you sort yourself out, just as he would back home. The closest of friendships may suffer when demands, which would cheerfully be accepted back home, are made in a different context. The friend may be living in a single room and, even if he has a flat, the arrival of a family is likely to lead to overcrowding. If the neighbours are hostile, they will be on the lookout for any cause for complaint, and so everyone has to be very quiet and creep in and out unseen. After the constant noise and talk and laughter back home, moving freely from one set of rooms to another, or chatting in the street or in the shade of a tree, what a strange way to find people living: complaining if a radio is too loud, passing you on the stairs without even a 'good morning', and above all 'keeping themselves to themselves'. The great British virtue of respect for a person's privacy can be felt as an icy blast added to the shock of the physical cold, never before experienced, which will hit a student arriving for the winter session.

The strains of bad housing need to be seen in the context of emotional isolation particularly for the newly arrived wife, who has never lived alone without the constant support of relatives and neighbours. She finds herself socially and physically cut-off in claustrophobic conditions. If she has small children she cannot safely go out of the house, even to a shop around the corner, without putting on their outdoor clothes and taking them along. The sun may shine deceptively in the winter but it gives out no heat. The room will be heated to what to most of us would seem an unbearable temperature, with no ventilation and with steaming windows in an attempt to recapture the warmth of home. Small wonder that in these circumstances a child is often left alone in the warm while mother braves the outside world to go shopping. It is only when a disaster occurs and a child is burnt that the true nature of the risk is understood. Alone means alone. At home any neighbour would be keeping an eye on the children and so this difficulty would not arise. Here a child could be screaming and no one would actually offer help. The best that might happen would be a call to the NSPCC!

**Prejudice**

It is, of course, against the law to put up a notice saying 'no coloureds', or even the typically British 'sorry, no coloureds', but this cannot prevent the experience of arriving on the doorstep to be told there is no vacancy thirty minutes after being assured on the phone that a flat was free. The student with an immaculate English accent or the one called Jones or Brown is particularly liable to have this sort of experience; this has already been well documented.[10] Sit almost anywhere in Africa with a group of Africans previously trained in Britain, reminiscing about life here, and they will invariably produce innumerable spontaneous accounts of these humiliating experiences. In retrospect they can laugh, and from the security of success in their own society, they can perhaps even forgive, but the pain is no less real at the time. It is not just the discomfort and the inconvenience of trailing the streets trying one address after another—given the present housing shortage, this a common experience for white people too—but the real demoralization of being in a situation where you are entirely at the mercy of other people's preconceived attitudes and can do absolutely nothing about them. 'It seems in this country it is as bad to have children as to be black', was the comment of one Nigerian searching for accommodation. If you not only have children but are also black then you really are at the bottom! The effects of prejudice should never be underestimated and cannot easily be shaken off. Because it is met with so frequently, even if in a veiled form, there comes a point when it is almost automatically assumed, and a white person has to go much more than half way to break through the defensive barriers that have been built up.

If prejudice is not always encountered ignorance is almost

universal. As Anna Craven pointed out when conducting her research among West African students in 1966-7, 'All West Africans know and feel strongly about the ignorance of the British public, even of educated individuals about Africa, Africans, their countries, communities, views and values, and what is more, the British seem not to care.'[11]

## Care of children

### *Working mothers*

Given the expectations of their own society, it is clear that very few wives are going to sit down at home, however decent their accommodation may be, and just look after their children. On the one hand, the young wife would be bored to desperation, and on the other, she would be regarded as idle and failing to take advantage of her opportunities. Whatever her personal wishes she will almost certainly have to work for economic reasons and in many cases will be the main financial support of the family. A study of West African families in London made in 1972 showed that 72 per cent of the wives were working full-time and only 12 per cent were studying full-time, but the majority of those working were also pursuing part-time studies.[12] Many West African women are employed in either cleaning or catering because the flexible hours allow them to pursue their studies at the same time; many are factory workers, and others work long hours in their own homes on piece-work, which is badly paid but at least allows them to have the children at home. The work a woman or her husband may be doing will probably give little indication of their skill or educational level. Obtaining white collar jobs is not easy and the anonymity of life in an English city means that a student will take any work he can get and not worry too much about status. It is unlikely, however, that the family back home will be informed of the true nature of his source of income.

Faced with financial difficulties, most West African women will work with enormous determination, often doing two jobs under exhausting conditions, rather than apply for social security benefits. A woman will choose to foster her children, even if a large proportion of her earnings goes to pay the foster mother, rather than endure the humiliation of drawing benefits to which she is fully entitled. The well-intentioned social worker who advises a mother to stay at home with the children while her husband goes out to work, ignores the fact that that would defeat the whole purpose of their stay in Britain and only prolong their difficulties. 'I know the children are suffering now', a mother will agree, 'but it is all for their own sake that we are doing this—once we go home life will be so much better for them.' There is a genuine ignorance of the damage that can be done during a child's early years.

*Fostering*

Because of the virtual impossibility of obtaining day nursery places, and the uncertainties and stresses involved in taking a child to a minder every day, West Africans have developed a pattern of sending their children to foster homes as a substitute for the care of the extended family.[13] This has created a whole new set of problems which are described by Vivien Biggs in Chapter five. Because of their attitudes to child care, usually based on their own experience of family life, African mothers are frequently regarded by social workers as completely irresponsible. Their pressures—to work, to study, to save money to buy consumer goods to take home, are not seen as justification for 'abandoning' their children. That a woman can love her child and still choose not to be involved in day-to-day caring for a period of several years, can only be understood in the context of the mother herself coming from a society where a child is frequently brought up by someone other than its biological mother. The social worker who is trying to analyse the mother's reasons for rejecting her child and the mother who is simply asking for a service to enable her to cope with the various demands on her time, are not communicating in a meaningful way. Parents feel no more guilt in asking for a foster home than do English parents who seek a boarding school for their children.

*Day care*

For the increasing number of mothers who are now rejecting fostering and seeking day care for their children, there are fresh problems.[14] Coming from a society where there are always willing child-minders, be they grandmothers, aunts or older siblings, or a relative brought specially from the village, it is not easy to appreciate the complexity of legislation relating to the care of children and not to regard it as yet another conspiracy of white society to make life more difficult for blacks. It is hard for a mother to accept that in this advanced country, with universal free education, a day nursery place is not available, and is only likely to be so if her whole family situation is on the verge of breakdown. In most African countries it is the élite families who send their children to nursery school and it is easy to conclude that prejudice is at the root of the failure to find a nursery place. A fortunate small minority may obtain places in nurseries run by colleges or attached to hostels, but such provision (the ideal answer to the problem) although increasing is still very rare. Almost all African parents seeking day care would prefer a nursery place for their child, not only because of the belief in the educational value of the nursery, but because of the enormous distrust of minders. For better or worse the mythology of the bad minder, as of the bad foster mother, is extensive. Every family knows stories of children being crowded twelve to a room, or being locked up all day while the minder goes to work, and is afraid that this could happen to their child. Whether justified or not such fears are real and present a serious barrier to the initial building of a relationship of confidence between the minder and the mother.

Problems arise because of the way child-minding services are usually organized by local authorities, although practice varies from one authority to another, and some important changes are taking place.[15] It is rare for a child to be 'placed' with an appropriate minder; the usual practice is for a mother to be given a list of names and addresses of approved minders with no indication of whether they have vacancies or not. The anxious mother goes from door to door and in nine cases out of ten is told that the minder has no vacancy. Given the gap between supply and demand, this is probably true, but for the exhausted mother who may be covering a pretty extensive area in her search, it is only too easy to conclude, as when flat hunting, that prejudice is the reason. There are of course very many minders who will only accept white children; some authorities may well eliminate these before handing addresses to the mother, others may not even be aware of how many of their minders do discriminate.[16] A mother who responds to an advertisement card in a shop window cannot of course know whether a minder is colour prejudiced, or even whether she is registered.

African parents are, unfortunately, not popular with minders who complain about a whole range of behaviour (similar criticisms are made by foster mothers). A common criticism is of arrogance: 'They order you about and think they are doing you a favour to let you look after their children' whereas, naturally enough, most minders like to feel that they are providing a valuable service as substitute mothers for which they will be appreciated. The mother, because she is a student, and her husband is an embryo doctor or teacher, and comes from a society with such a high regard for education, perceives herself as belonging to the élite (and indeed may have done before coming to Britain). By virtue of being black, she is perceived by the minder as being near the bottom of the social hierarchy, or if the minder is a West Indian, as being 'just one of us' so why should she put on airs? Often her superiority is only a form of bravado when everything seems stacked against her.

Then there is the tendency to haggle over the fees: 'bargaining over their own children' is how it is seen, and this is also a common problem faced by foster mothers. Fixing of standard fees by the social worker would do a lot to avoid unpleasantness here. All too often the minder feels bullied into accepting a reduction in order to placate the mother, who basically finds it difficult to accept that one has to pay so much money just for looking after children, but naturally resents this and holds it against the mother. It is common for the mother not only to travel a long way from her home to that of the minder, but then to be faced with another long journey to college or to work, often right across the city, because it is rare for accommodation, college and job to coincide. This means the child is brought early and collected late, not through a wish to be rid of the child for as long as possible, but because of the sheer mechanics of the situation. The mother may well face all the stress of rush hour travel on top of her other worries, and the difficulty of taking a small child to a minder under these conditions is often given as a reason for preferring a foster home. Children are often brought to the minder, or to the nursery, if the mother has been lucky enough to obtain a nursery place, when they are not well and ought to be kept at home. It is hard for a white person to understand the effort an African will feel she has to make to hold on to a job. Whereas an English mother may well take two or three days off if her child is sick, without too much worry, an African will be conscious that she will be quickly labelled as unreliable and may lose her job. She does not have to be as efficient as the girls she is working with, but more so. If she is in a position of real responsibility, the situation is worse and the pressures placed on the mother can be severe. Often her employer is not aware that she has a child at all and, whether her fears are real or imagined, she is convinced that she will not keep her job if it is known she has a young child. This applies particularly to nurses; they will rarely reveal the existence of children when they apply for training, and therefore they, more than any other group, may feel compelled to foster, even if a husband is willing to co-operate by caring for the child when his wife is on night duty. Concealing the existence of her children at work when other staff are chatting normally about their families, is an additional source of strain to the young mother.

In both child-minding and fostering situations fundamental conflicts may arise because of the white mother substitute's negative view of the child's parents and their culture. The child minder's view of Africa is, not surprisingly, gained from television. This can give the impression that it is a continent where war and starvation are widespread; where any peaceful interludes are occupied by bizarre tribal dancing and other exotic activities; and where wild animals are to be found in abundance. (My own children, who spent their early years in Nigeria, soon started inventing stories of lions, crocodiles and elephants to impress their friends in England, as they realized what was expected of them. It would have been too dull to only talk about lizards, mosquitoes and ants!) The minders' negative attitudes are reinforced by the different approach to child-rearing of West Africans as analysed by June Ellis in Chapter three, and by what the minder regards as a demonstrable lack of affection on the part of the parents.

*The social worker's approach*

African parents going to a social worker for help can easily become confused and disheartened by the non-directive approach. They are usually looking for straightforward advice of the kind they might receive from the family back home, as when a couple would be 'told' what to do in cases of marital conflict. Some will prefer a solicitor's approach to that of a social worker and get him to draw up a list of conditions that both parties will adhere to. Many African parents quickly learn to adapt to the social worker's perceptions and produce a story that will lead to the necessary help being forthcoming. A wife may 'desert' her husband in order to obtain a day nursery place, but she will be very close at hand, and if found in the house when a social worker calls, will be introduced as a good friend who is helping out. The case of a young Ghanaian wife who told the social worker that her child was illegitimate and she wanted it adopted, when all she needed was temporary help, illustrates the misconceptions that can so easily develop. She was very naive but was acting on the advice of old-timers who thought they knew how to work the system.

This adaptation to what is expected presents a challenge to the social worker to seek to understand the real need behind what can so often be regarded as 'a tissue of lies', a challenge which the hard-pressed and over-burdened worker may not find easy. Detecting the symptoms of impending breakdown in someone from another culture is never simple; too often it is only when a child has been burnt when left alone, a mother has a mental breakdown or a father has committed suicide because of worry and frustration, that the necessary help is forthcoming. The balance between the negative approach to the parents as irresponsible, and the over-helpful one that may lead a parent to feel a child is better off 'in care', is precarious. It can only be maintained if a constant attempt is made to see the situation not only in terms of life in England, but also with traditional behaviour patterns and expectations in mind.

The story of Carol, a young Nigerian schoolgirl mother, illustrates the dilemma. She was referred to social services by her school, and the social worker who interviewed Carol and her mother found the mother very censorious of her daughter, who appeared to her to be ruining her educational prospects. The social worker identified with Carol's aspirations and with her need to establish herself and her baby in face of her mother's severity. She recommended that the baby should be received into care and placed with an understanding foster mother so that Carol could visit regularly and build up her own relationship with her baby away from her domineering mother. Carol's mother was totally bewildered by this new situation in which she had no role. In spite of her anger at her daughter's behaviour she would have willingly cared for the child. She could not understand how her own grandchild could be handed to a total stranger, without her being involved in any way. In this situation, the family if left to themselves, would have coped perfectly well. Once the case had been referred by a well-intentioned welfare officer, respect for the young girl's wishes, a criterion that would have been irrelevant back home, became the dominating factor and led to the virtual break-up of the family. The social worker's intervention and misinterpretation of their relationship led to the increasing estrangement of Carol from her mother.

### *The children*

The question is invariably raised by those who become involved with the problems these families face of why so many West African couples have children while they are still students in Britain. Many parents do in fact leave older children behind, and by far the largest number of African children in Britain are born here, not brought here. The fact that, in a number of cases, the family is truncated and the older siblings are not there to assist with the care of the younger ones, is part of the problem.

Given the significance of children to the stability of a West African marriage, it is hard for a newly married couple to resist family pressure even if they themselves might have preferred to wait until they had completed their studies before starting a family. Obviously it would be helpful for advice to be given about family planning before students come here rather than subjecting them to the sort of pressures that imply 'we don't want your babies here', but it may be the older generation who need to be convinced that, unless their sons and daughters can concentrate on their studies without the worries of parenthood, they are unlikely to succeed. Some parents feel that to have a baby born in Britain and for it to spend its infancy here, will give it a far greater chance of survival. (Though the infant mortality rate is steadily dropping in African countries as health services improve, it is still high.) Others may feel the child will benefit particularly in the development of linguistic skills.

Many parents do decide to send their children who have been born in Britain, back to their own parents and this is usually much encouraged by their families, who may feel it will provide an incentive to the parents to come home as soon as they can. The main cause of concern is then that of the best age for the move; most parents prefer to wait until the children are two years old because at that age the child will be more resistant to illness, but from the emotional point of view, adaptation would no doubt be easier during the first few months. In attempting to advise on this issue one needs to know something of the standard of care the child will receive in the family home and the nearness to adequate medical facilities. At the Ibadan seminar on the West African child in Great Britain a Ghanaian doctor suggested that it would be valuable to have a register of very young children returning without their mothers, as they might be particularly at risk, and the receiving family would benefit from support.

## Marriage

African mothers in Britain have to cope with very severe pressures. The roles of breadwinner, student and mother, combined with the isolation from the support of the extended family, and the hostility of British society, can create grave tensions which may lead to breakdown. For the men, the process of adaptation is in many ways easier, because their work or study presents them with an environment which does not seriously conflict with their accepted behaviour patterns. In the home, however, they are likely to be faced with new issues; many men confess how much they enjoy the chance of being closely involved with their very young children, in a way which would not be possible back home, where the idea of a man changing nappies or giving the baby its bottle would be unheard of. Many do respond to this new situation by helping their wives with the domestic chores and the success of the couple's adaptation to life in Britain probably depends to a large extent on how much the man is prepared to move away from his traditional role. The man is often the one who will make contacts with officialdom, will take a child to the clinic, will visit the school and so forth. He is particularly likely to do this when his command of English is better than that of his wife. In some cases a man may even request a foster home for a child when his wife is anxious to keep the child with her. Couples may also have difficulties resulting from decisions over finance; conflict over the spending of the wife's wages can cause serious disagreement. A husband may be used to his wife having her own income which she can spend as she chooses, but not to her being the major breadwinner on whom he is dependent.

Some West African men feel threatened by British attitudes to women's rights particularly where children are concerned. The husband is afraid that if he beats his wife to keep her in order or remind her who is the boss—a pattern of behaviour readily sanctioned at home—she may run to a social worker; if convincing enough, she will be helped and given somewhere to go with the children. The idea that in the case of breakdown the father might himself wish to take over responsibility for the care of the children and send them to his mother or sister to be cared for, as he almost certainly would if he came from a patrilineal society, is not usually considered. In cases of marital breakdown it seems rare for a serious effort to be made to assess the father's wishes where young children are concerned.[17] The case history of Julian shows how a father may be able to provide a very satisfactory home for his child, and this possibility should always be taken into consideration. One boy grew up in a children's home and, although his English mother spent most of her time in mental hospital and was clearly unable to cope with her son, no attempt had been made to contact the Nigerian father, although he was known to be in London. By the time the boy himself was old enough to start asking about his father and considering the possibility of going to Nigeria to look for him, there were no records beyond the father's name on the birth certificate, to help trace him.

For a woman coming from a matrilineal society where the young wife has had to move completely away from her own family and identify with her husband's way of life against all the traditions of her upbringing, the strains are even more acute. In Chapter two we saw how in the patrilineal society the wife is entrusted to her husband and his family; in spite of the links she may still keep with her own family, she is committed to him and to a life with him. The matrilineal wife on the other hand traditionally remains in the security of her own home, depends very much on her mother and brothers for support; and invests her future, and that of her children, in her own family. Even if she is lucky enough to have relatives in England, such a girl finds herself in a far more exposed situation and, if things go wrong her commitment to the marriage may be less, so that she is more likely to leave her husband and set up house on her own or with another man.

Only one study has been done which compares the adaptation of West African student couples from matrilineal and patrilineal societies.[18] Unfortunately the sample studied in depth was very small, but even so its findings are of interest: the patrilineal group of Ibo students showed a much readier adaptation to joint conjugal roles on the western middle-class pattern than the matrilineal

Ashanti who tended to maintain their separate roles very clearly. In both groups it was clear that tension was markedly less where roles were closely shared and when decision-making was a joint activity. If the father helps with the care of the children, undertakes some of the domestic chores, assists with the shopping and shares the decisions on how to spend the family income, the chances are that the family will be better adjusted than when traditional roles are strictly maintained. But the process of re-adaptation to life in Africa may prove more difficult for such couples. Many wives now home in Africa look back with nostalgia to the days when their husbands discussed everything with them and shared their daily life more closely. The women still seek the companionship the men no longer feel the need for. It is easy for the man to slip back into the old pattern without realizing the loss to his wife. Marriages that have survived all the difficulties of life in Britain may still collapse when the couple return home and are no longer held together by a common struggle.

An awareness of the uncertainty surrounding their own future and a recognition of the 'polygamous' nature of men in general, are factors strengthening the determination of wives to qualify in their own right. Some men, once they have completed their own courses are ready to go home and totally disregard the promises made to their wives to stay for another year and work to allow the wives the chance to qualify. It is not unknown for a man to go ahead to look for a job, promising to send for his wife as soon as he has fixed something up. Years later the wife may still be waiting, but will maintain her dignity and self-respect by regarding herself as a student in some form, even if this only involves evening classes once a week.

Maintaining family unity in such conditions which seem the norm for so many African families in Britain is a permanent struggle. When they finally return home most former students think the effort was worth while, but one cannot help asking what are the consequences for their children, and whether it would be possible to relieve some of the pressures these families face.

## Notes

1 'Beento' is a common nickname for those who have been to Europe.

2 British Council Statistics of Overseas Students in Britain 1975/6. These statistics produced annually give a detailed analysis by country of origin, college attended, course of study, etc.

3 E. M. Goody and C. L. Muir, 'Factors Related to the Delegation of Parental Roles among West Africans in London', unpublished report, Committee for the Social and Political Sciences, University of Cambridge, 1972.

4 *The Situation of Married Overseas Students in the UK,* pilot study, UKOSA, 1972.

5 There are now thirteen universities in Nigeria, some of them very newly established. In Ghana there are three and in Sierra Leone two.

6 Peter Lloyd, *Power and Independence: Urban Africans' Perception of Social Inequality,* Routledge & Kegan Paul, 1974, p. 119.

7 Wig-making, for instance, can be a highly lucrative profession, and in Nigeria one sees a large number of 'domestic science' establishments, run in very small premises, by a proprietress 'trained in Britain'. 'London trained' dressmakers abound throughout West Africa, as do caterers supplying wedding cakes and other specialities.

8 Budgeting for life in Britain is difficult to do accurately even with the best advice. Transport costs are rarely adequately allowed for, nor is heating. It is always more expensive for a foreign student than a local one who knows the cheapest ways of surviving. The temptations of easy hire purchase can be difficult to resist.

9 Both *In the Ditch* and *Second-Class Citizen* by Buchi Emecheta give graphic descriptions of housing conditions, but the case files of the CSCS are just as horrific.

10 W. W. Daniel, *Racial Discrimination in England,* Harmondsworth, Penguin Books, 1968, part four.

11 Anna Craven, *West Africans in London,* Institute of Race Relations, 1968, p. vii.

12 Goody and Muir, op. cit.

13 A substantial part of the material used in this section was published in *Social Work Today,* vol. 7, no. 9, 1976, 'Culture Clashes and the Childminder' by Pat Stapleton.

14 *Child Minding in London,* a report by the London Council of Social Service, 1977, gives a clear picture of the variations in provision and policy in the different boroughs.

15 *Who Minds? A Study of Working Mothers and Childminding in Ethnic Minority Communities,* CRC Publications, 1975.

16 Some authorities will not register a minder who discriminates on racial grounds, but as with fostering it is usually accepted that this is an area where personal views have to be allowed for.

17 I visited a family in Nigeria who were preparing to receive their daughter and her three children, after the breakdown of her marriage in England. In spite of the fact that they regarded the husband as a thoroughly unsatisfactory character, and the British courts had awarded custody of all three children to their mother, the family were making it clear that they felt the husband was really entitled to keep at least one of the children if he really wanted to. They also made it quite clear that they would welcome the husband's parents keeping in close contact with the children. They had no quarrel with them.

18 Goody and Muir, op. cit.

Chapter Five

# Private fostering

*Vivien Biggs*

> 'The unkind foster mother neglects your child; the kind one steals it', said a West African mother whose children had been fostered.
>
> 'Why did she have a baby, give him to me so young, allow him to become part of our family, and then ask for him back—now, when he is four years old, and is going to find it so difficult to leave us?' asked a foster mother.

These two points of view epitomize the major problems of children privately placed in foster homes without the agency of a social services department. West African parents approach such an arrangement with a very different cultural background from the British foster mother. They have many hopeful expectations of successfully sharing their child with another family. They cannot believe that a good motherly woman will either neglect or try to 'steal' a child. On the other hand the foster mother approaches the transaction with quite different hopes, possibly seeing it as a backdoor to adoption, and almost certainly with the idea of building a close loving relationship with a child whom another mother seems to have rejected. Robert Holman likened the private fostering system to a market: 'Parents require a service, foster parents offer a service—the two sides contact each other, negotiate the terms, and the goods (the children) change hands.'[1] This is a free-for-all trade, with remarkably few restraints, in which the children are the victims of adult bargaining. There are no written contracts, scarcely any legal requirements, and the whole business is bedevilled by misunderstandings, misconceptions and double-dealing on both sides.

Children are taken into the care of a local authority most often because the family has completely broken down. They are in need of substitute parents, because their own parents are quite unable to look after them, as is explained in Chapter six. The majority of children privately placed in foster homes in Britain are West African, and a family breakdown is seldom the cause of their need for substitute care. It is, however, important to consider why these parents place their children in foster homes, and why the foster parents offer their services for this particular kind of fostering. We need to know how private placements differ from those made for children in the care of the local authorities, what quality of care the children receive, and how the relationships between all the people involved develop.

## The parents' cultural background and student problems

In West Africa a child has many 'fathers' and 'mothers' in addition to his biological parents. He is seen as a child of the family, and is often cared for by relatives, as is described by Pat Stapleton in Chapter two. But wherever he lives, there is no confusion in anyone's mind about whose child he is. The practice of fostering is sometimes used to give the child an opportunity to benefit from a higher standard of living, or learn special skills. Whereas British families only resort to looking for a foster home in a crisis, West African families regard it as a normal response to the need for help in looking after their children.

The majority of West African parents placing their children in foster homes in Britain are students, who have great difficulty in looking after their children themselves. As has been pointed out in Chapter four, they often live in very poor accommodation, with the added strain of at least one parent studying and their financial position is usually precarious, as nearly all are self-financed. Either both parents study, and both have part-time jobs, or (more commonly) the father is a full-time student, and the mother works full-time to support the family, but also studies part-time. Occasionally their timetables can be manipulated so that one parent is always at home to care for the children, but this is by no means always possible—and indeed not all fathers are prepared to play this role. Many West African mothers are student nurses, and cannot have their children with them because they are living in nurses' homes.

The relative expense of having their children daily-minded is also a real factor in the decision of many families to choose fostering as a solution. A child-minder cares for a child for five nine-hour days, providing only a midday snack lunch, and sending home all the dirty washing for the mother to do. A foster mother, on the other hand relieves the mother of all care of the child for seven twenty-four-hour days for about two-thirds of the child-minder's fee. There are extra expenses in travelling to visit a child in a foster home in the country, of course, but a foster home is still much cheaper than a daily-minder.

## Foster parents' motives

Holman found in his sample that the motives of foster mothers were many and mixed, but that only 3 per cent were financially motivated.[2] Certainly in my experience the maternal drive of foster mothers is often unusually strong, and in a meeting of foster mothers many of them said that they could not sleep at night unless they had a baby in the room with them. Many of them are not qualified or experienced in any work other than mothering. In this they have often been very successful with their own children, and have been praised by friends and relatives for their ability with young children. They see themselves as mothers above all. Some, on the other hand, are frustrated, childless and unable to adopt for some reason, but feel they would be good mothers, if only someone would provide them with babies with whom to prove it. All certainly profess great love for young children. A number of private foster mothers say that they want to 'help someone in need'. Many say that they like black children because they are easier—presenting fewer problems with feeding and sleeping. Most prefer private placements because the system is free from controls, form-filling, assessments, and 'interfering' social workers. Moreover it is much quicker to arrange a private placement, and a strong-minded foster mother feels that she is in charge of the situation. An advertisement is answered, the parents visit, she lays down her terms, and (if they agree) the child soon arrives.

There are many good private foster homes, and happy private fostering arrangements. Some of the foster parents find themselves able to relate very well to the West African parents. Particularly if they come from large families themselves, they can adopt the 'sharing' concept quite easily; they welcome the visiting parents as they would welcome their own relatives, and the West African family sometimes find that their child's foster home is the only British home where they can relax and meet British people on easy, equal terms. In these cases the child moves easily from one set of parents to the other; he feels equally at ease in either home, and when the time comes for him to leave the foster home, he goes happily, very often returning for short holidays as long as he is in Britain. I have known several cases where young African men and women return to their British childhood foster homes to lodge while they pursue their higher education.

There is another group of relatively successful foster mothers—

those who are more 'professional'. They are usually extremely efficient, and are often trained nursery nurses. They give good material care, recognize the need for the child to maintain a good relationship with his parents, and strive to achieve this. But these foster mothers deliberately control their emotional involvement, and often the degree of detachment is such that neither child nor parents get much affection or friendship from the arrangement. In such a home, a foster child may well be aware of his second-class status.

In unsatisfactory fostering placements the material care is usually well below the standard which a local authority would demand for the children in their care. In fact many private foster mothers have had their applications to become registered foster mothers turned down by local authorities. In Kent where there had been a long tradition of fostering West African children, there were thought to be about 1,000 West African children in about 600 private foster homes in 1975—and it is estimated by local authority social workers that not more than half of these would meet the required standard for a registered foster home.[3] A West African mother once asked me to visit a foster home for her. The prospective foster mother had answered her advertisement seeking a foster home for her child; I called and with difficulty persuaded the foster mother to let me in. The front room was dark, with the curtains drawn, but I could just see one child strapped into a pram, rocking it dangerously back and forth; another was tied to the leg of a chair. The door handle on the inside had been removed; there was an oil heater in the middle of the floor. I went at once to the local authority social services department where I was told that they knew of the foster home, but that when they had visited they had always found everything reasonably satisfactory but that the social worker had always made an appointment before visiting. Apparently the pressure of work was so great that a wasted call to a foster home could not be afforded, should the foster mother have been out. This is an obvious case of neglect, but there are others where the arrangement is not a good one for the child, although at first sight it is not easy to identify the reasons. The following three examples will be familiar to most social workers:

Mrs Brown is a widow of fifty-eight, who lives in her own house on a small modern estate with her single son of thirty-two. Her house and garden are neat, and she fosters one West African child. She gives this child her entire attention, taking great pleasure in knitting for him, taking him to the clinic, preparing his favourite food, reading to him, and nursing him when he has the slightest ailment. Her own son is very fond of him too, and they both take a tremendous interest in his progress and development. 'His mother can't understand him as we do', says Mrs Brown. 'She hardly knows him, and he is very frightened of her.' This child is gradually being alienated from his mother, and insidiously taught to believe that she is inadequate. Mrs Brown urges him to be good when his mother comes, but consoles him: 'It's only for a little while. You must behave yourself, or she might take you away.' He grows more and more afraid of his mother, and the idea of going to live with her becomes very alarming. When the time comes, either his parents will snatch him for fear of the consequences of giving warning of their intentions, or before they can do so, Mrs Brown will apply to the court for wardship on the basis that the child will be most unhappy with his parents.

Mrs Jackson, a woman with five children of her own, usually fosters at least two West African children. She prides herself on having a full and noisy house. She lives in a council house, which is very untidy and rather grubby. The garden is full of broken toys, and the house is strewn with clothes. Mrs Jackson is very jovial with adults, but irritable with the children; she shouts a good deal at the older ones, and slaps the smaller ones. All the children are very whiny, and most of them seem to have running noses. She maintains that she fosters because she loves children, but seems to look forward to the time when the African children will return to their parents, saying that she hopes the next ones will be less trouble. The foster children in this home receive practically no affection, and no stimulation. There is real racial prejudice against them, and it is hard to know why Mrs Jackson fosters at all. Perhaps it is because she treasures her image locally of a woman with an enormous family, or because she is considered amongst her neighbours to be the local expert on Africans and West Indians. Perhaps too, she is satisfying some need to seek for sympathy through overwork, and caring for other people's difficult children.

By contrast with these two foster mothers, Mrs Jones has a warm and comfortable home. Large and loving she welcomes the West African parents of her two foster children when they visit. She calls them by their first names, and takes an interest in the progress of their studies, rejoicing in their successes, and expressing motherly concern for them at examination times. To her foster children, she always refers to their parents as 'Mummy and Daddy', and speaks admiringly of their struggles to gain qualifications. The West African mother bathes and feeds her children when she visits, and sometimes cooks an African meal for the Jones family. Mrs Jones often talks to her foster children of their future in Africa, and emphasizes what an adventure it will be. She even carries on a correspondence with the children's grandparents in Africa, telling them of the children's progress, and learning something of their way of life, of which she can then talk to the children. Mr and Mrs Jones plan to go on holiday to Nigeria when Mr Jones retires to visit the many Nigerian foster children for whom they have cared, and with whom they now correspond. A child in this home gains enormously from the loving care he receives, not only from Mrs Jones, but also from Mr Jones who plays a large part in handling and playing with him. Even more important, such a child is able to return to his parents without trauma, and with great respect for them, when the time comes.

## Private fostering and the local authorities

As shown in Chapter six, the safeguards for children privately placed in foster homes compare poorly with those for children in the care of the local authority. The Boarding-Out Regulations 1955, and the Children Acts of 1958 and 1975 all demand that material standards must be satisfactory in local authority fostering and that foster parents must be suitable according to laid-down criteria. Over and above this, the local authority social worker is required to make a series of visits to assess the suitability and motivation of the foster parents, and a great deal of consideration is given to matching the child with the foster home. Finally, once placed, there is a statutory duty upon the social worker to supervise the placement, to seek to develop a good relationship with the foster parents, the natural parents and the fostered child, and to visit the foster home at frequent and specified intervals.

No such safeguards characterize the private placement of a child in a foster home. These children, placed privately and probably in the worst conditions, have the least chance of professional help. The only control which a local authority has over private fostering arrangements lies in the duty of the foster mother to inform the local authority when she intends to take a child, and when the child leaves her home. While he is there, the social worker must visit, where she thinks it 'appropriate'. In effect, this is a discretionary visit, which in a busy office with a generic caseload does not often receive high priority. In addition, these children are not matched with the foster parents, they are not gradually introduced into their new homes, and very little information about their habits, needs and behaviour is given by the parents to the foster parents. When West African children are placed in foster homes there is often very little communication between the sets of parents: the child is brought to the home with a few clothes, a fee is agreed upon, and the child is handed over. The story of the child being dumped on the sofa, and the parents departing within a few minutes and without a backward glance is one most social workers have heard. Many social workers, health visitors, and doctors, if they see that the arrangement is not a satisfactory one for the child, will urge the foster mother to return him to his parents, not realizing that he will be placed in another foster home as soon as his parents can find one. The parents' problems have not been eased and their response is still the same: they assume that there can be a happy solution for themselves and the child in finding a good foster mother.

Some children are re-fostered many times—up to seven times a year is not uncommon—and of course this presents many problems for the child. He has to adjust to different ways of being handled, he has to cope with different family tensions, he even has to eat different food at different times. The child who has been moved several times begins to present behaviour problems, and as a result is often rejected by each new foster mother as 'too difficult'. Moreover, if the parents continue to use the same method of choosing a foster home, and show the same lack of discrimination, and the same inability to communicate, the chances are that the same mistakes will be made over and over again, with all the attendant damage to the child.

Dr Alexina McWhinnie, at a seminar in Nigeria in 1975 on the African child in Great Britain, said:[4]

> In practice social workers in a local authority setting are unsure of their role. They feel that they come in too late to make effective assessments and effective prohibitions. Their role in supervision is ill-defined.

Many social workers, somewhat concerned about the minimal supervision they can give to private placements in foster homes, justify their lack of action by saying:

> It is not a very bad home, and after all the parents must think it is all right, and I suppose they are visiting, so I only call when I am passing and have time.

They feel that because it is a private arrangement, the parents should be in control of the situation. One senior social worker said to me,

> After all, they are not *our* children [meaning children of local families], and we have never met their parents. If the children leave, we will have the problem of supporting the grieving foster mother. It's less trouble to let things ride, if the children are not seriously at risk.

There is a clear double standard at work here. Also, in the experience of the Commonwealth Students' Children Society, social workers would sometimes like a child removed from a foster home because it is unsatisfactory, but are unable to prevent the private placement of another child, because there is not sufficient evidence to take the foster mother to court and get her prohibited from fostering. The regulations outlined in Chapter six are difficult to implement, because of the necessity to prove the unsuitability of the home in law, and the local authority is reluctant to go to the court unless they are sure of success. So, in fact what happens is that the parents are pressed to take their child away from a foster home, but the parents know and the foster mother knows that there is nothing to prevent her taking another child immediately afterwards.

## Finding a private foster home

Among West Africans in London and other large cities of the United Kingdom there is a fund of information about private fostering—much of it inaccurate. However, it is well known, correctly, that unless a mother is unmarried or physically or mentally ill there is little chance of her getting help from her social services department. Occasionally a welfare officer at a college or a priest or a health visitor will help, but more commonly these people, and social workers too, confront West African student parents who are seeking advice with a complete lack of understanding of their culture. Although they cannot be expected to have expert knowledge, many nevertheless display a remarkable lack of sensitivity to differences in cultural background of their clients. With a complete misunderstanding of West African attitudes, they offer such advice as: 'Why don't you stay at home and look after your child?', and make judgments on past decisions such as: 'Why do you have babies if you are not going to look after them?' or 'Why did you get married and have children while you are still studying?' As can be seen from Chapter two these attitudes are questioning a way of life which the West African parents consider to be not only normal, but quite proper. Many West African parents are driven to despair by the lack of insight on the part of social workers, and sometimes appear arrogant and aggressive towards young social workers, whom they see as inferior—being inexperienced and childless. A young person, and more particularly an unmarried person, is not seen to be qualified, however highly trained, to give fundamental advice on planning his life to an older one with a family.

And so West African parents searching for help in caring for their children use methods of finding a foster home which have been well tried. Sometimes friends and relatives can recommend a foster mother known to them, but it is also well known that advertisements in the *Nursery World* or in local papers in the Home Counties usually receive many replies. Sometimes even social workers will recommend advertising to desperate parents, although there has been a welcome move on the part of some local papers not to accept such advertisements before first consulting the social services department. Both the British Association of Social Workers and the Association of Directors of Social Services have supported attempts by the Commonwealth Students' Children Society to encourage legislation to prohibit private advertisements by people seeking foster homes for their children. The National Council of Women passed a resolution in 1977 urging the government to implement Clause 97 of the Children Act 1975 prohibiting such advertisements.

The Commonwealth Students' Children Society answers all advertisements from those seeking foster homes for their children in the *Nursery World*, and, as well as offering a counselling service, asks parents to let the Society know who answers their advertisements. The same women appear on their lists, over and over again, year after year, and over 50 per cent of them are foster mothers who are regarded as unsatisfactory by local authority social services departments. If advertising were to be prohibited, these women would have no easy market in which to find children. At the same time West African parents who could manage to look after their children themselves with the help of day care would turn less readily to fostering. The knowledge that an advertisement will elicit some twenty replies, compared with the difficulty of finding a daily-minder, makes looking for a foster mother an easy option.

Assessing a foster home is a very skilled task, requiring all the expertise of experienced and sensitive social workers. Even they can sometimes fail to judge accurately the foster mother's ability to give a child love and security but to stop short at the point of possessiveness. A West African mother with no training and a desperate need to find a foster home for her baby is very handicapped. She may never get beyond the hallway of a prospective foster home. Speaking a foreign language, she is trying to assess the stability and motivation of someone from another culture. Most of all, she *wants* to believe the foster mother's claim to be maternal, kind and experienced, and when the foster mother offers to take the baby at a low fee, she hopes that she is indeed like the loving relative she would have found at home in Africa to look after her child. The West African idea of a good foster mother is often quite different from that of a British social worker. African parents tend to look for an older woman who has cared for many children, as they see her in the role of a grandmother. They are seldom concerned that the child has other children of his own age to play with, but they are pleased if he is taught good manners of a rather old-fashioned kind by British standards. They like him to be big and advanced and are particularly worried if he is not forward at school. They do not place the same emphasis as a British social worker may do on the formation of an emotional bond between their child and the foster mother. In fact, if they see this develop, they may look upon it as a threat to their own relationship with him. Furthermore, as June Ellis has pointed out in Chaper three, West African attitudes to child-rearing do not stress the child's need for constructive play. West African parents therefore do not place much value on the degree of stimulation in play which a foster mother can give. In these things, they often find a social worker's standards and priorities hard to understand, as she finds theirs.

The anxiety that a British mother might feel at sharing her child with another woman is largely, if not entirely absent in a West African mother, conditioned as she is by her cultural background. Dr Helen Ware says,[5]

> In an African context all children are in a sense everybody's children, or at least the concern of a great number and range of relatives, and there is much less stress upon the individual mother's role in the socialization of the child.

So if the British foster mother seems to be suitable at first sight, West African parents will readily place their children with her, and plan to come back to see how they are in a week or two. Their first concern then is for their physical well-being, as they do not anticipate any difficulties in sharing them with a reasonable and loving foster mother. For example, Mr Adeyinka, a Nigerian father, said, after a serious breakdown in fostering,

> When we took the baby to her she told us that she had brought up five healthy children of her own. She showed us many pictures of other foster children she had had, and she said that her charge was very low because she did it for the love of the children and not because she wanted to make a profit. Her house was very clean and it seemed to be a nice neighbourhood.

He did not recognize in her the symptoms of an hysterical need for a child. This foster mother was known to the local authority, her doctor and the local psychiatric hospital as a neurotic woman, who was very manipulative with her whole family, and whose need for a child had not been satisfied, because the local authority had turned her down as a registered foster mother, and her children would not allow her to care for their children. The result was a series of depressions and suicide attempts. Mr Adeyinka placed his child, but within months it became clear to him that he was being alienated from his son, and when he announced his intention of removing him, the foster mother reacted violently, threatening to kill herself and the child. Mr Adeyinka was forced to go unannounced and 'snatch' the child from her.

**Differing perceptions of mothering roles**

The African mother sees the fostering arrangement as a temporary solution to her problems of caring for her child while she is working and studying. At the same time she hopes her child will benefit from the standards in a British home, and she may express this by saying, 'He is with you for his education.' The foster mother on the other hand may hope that the child is to be with her for many years; she may be desperate for a child of her own, and to her these words bring hope. She understands them to mean that he will stay until the end of his schooling, by the end of which she hopes that he will not want to leave her. Many student parents will place the child with a foster mother and either not state how long he is to stay with her or, speaking metaphorically, say, 'I give you my child', which may be interpreted by the hopeful foster mother as some form of adoption.

There is a fear in some West African parents' minds that to state plainly that the arrangement is to be limited to a year or two will mean that the foster mother will not care as well for the child as she would if she thought he was to be there for many years, possibly all his childhood. Very often therefore, parents will deliberately deceive the foster mother and give wrong or misleading information about their long-term plans. Sometimes, in addition, they do not wish to be too specific, even in their own minds, about the length of the term of the fostering arrangement. To make definite statements about plans and ambitions may seem to be 'tempting fate'; moreover the African traditionally does not make firm plans. As Pat Stapleton has explained in Chapter two, the flexibility of life and hospitality in West Africa have produced a code of behaviour in which no one expects plans to be specific or binding.

The West African mother, likening the arrangement to one she might make with a relative, presumes she will still have 'control' of the child. She expects ultimately to make decisions about his care, where he lives, and generally to direct his life and future. She sees herself and her husband as behaving perfectly responsibly in pursuing their studies at all costs, considering this to be in the long-term interests of their child. The British foster mother, however, understands the situation quite differently. She very often thinks that the West African parents have opted out of caring for their child, and are more interested in obtaining their qualifications. She believes that she, and not his African mother, is in full control of the child, and may hope that the arrangement is indeed a backdoor to adoption. She intends to build a one-to-one mothering relationship with the child without interference from his own mother. A foster mother said, 'They won't pay for her ballet classes or even come to see her perform', to which the African parents responded, 'What interest do we have in ballet? If it amuses Mrs Robinson to have her taught this strange dancing, we have no objection, but she must pay for it herself.'

These misunderstandings are in a sense inevitable, given the differing expectations of the contract between the natural mother and the foster mother. The two women, moreover, expect to play different roles, and one of the areas of greatest conflict is in the arrangements for the parents to visit their child. The West African mother, visiting the foster home in the same spirit in which she would visit her child in a relative's home, may well bring friends to see her baby, and make an outing of it, but not concern herself over doing anything for the child. She feels that she has entrusted this child to the foster mother, and can see no point in interfering with the care he is receiving. She often does not show obvious affection towards her child, which would be quite acceptable in the circumstances at home in Africa, but the foster mother may interpret it as uncaring, heartless behaviour. Also, with an African attitude to hospitality, the West African family can see no problem in four or five people instead of two coming to see the child. The foster parents see this as an invasion of their privacy, and a gross presumption on their hospitality. They may well think that their responsibility ends with the care of the child, and although they can accept unwillingly the need of the parents to visit their child, they may only barely tolerate this. The arrival of a party of people to visit a child they are growing to regard as their own, can be a very unwelcome sight.

Very occasionally, a young African mother with her first baby is aware of her inexperience in handling a new baby; at home in Africa her mother or mother-in-law would probably look after the child and instruct the young mother in the first few weeks of the baby's life. Even with a second baby she might not be trusted by the family with the sole charge of it. In Britain, unsupported by the extended family, she may be very conscious of the foster mother's much greater knowledge and experience, and be very reluctant to do anything for her child. She is afraid that he will cry and reject her, that the foster mother will witness the rejection, and so she may even refuse to hold her baby. The foster mother with little understanding of the young woman's fears and need for motherly help, interprets her unwillingness to handle her child as another symptom of her lack of interest and her irresponsibility.

Sometimes, on the other hand, an African mother may see her role as supplying the African element in the child's care—giving him a ceremonial scrubbing, or plaiting her little girl's hair in an African style. Both can give offence to the foster mother, who resents the rough handling the child receives, and feels that she is left with an unhappy child after an unpleasant few hours for everyone. Unless some third party is able to help to explain the differences in behaviour and habits between the two women there can be a serious rift, in which the main sufferer is the child. A foster mother sometimes complains that Africans laugh when some very important problem is being discussed. She does not know that in West Africa uproarious laughter is a common response to uncertainty, tension or embarrassment and quite misinterprets their laughter as a minimizing or dismissal of the difficulty. On the other hand West African parents often take their baby's progress very seriously, and want him to be advanced, to sit up early and walk early. They may try to make the baby stand or walk when they visit, or complain that he is not progressing fast enough. Foster mothers resent this and see it as criticism of them. West African parents are sometimes puzzled by the lack of discipline in British homes. They want their children to be quiet and obedient, and think they are encouraged to be cheeky by the foster mother. They become very anxious, they complain, and the foster mother is offended. The amount a child is encouraged to do for himself may cause the natural mother to feel that the foster mother is not doing the job for which she is paid. The idea of a 'routine', dear to the hearts of so many British mothers, may be anathema to the mother from another culture. I remember a foster mother, a trained nursery nurse, who struggled to achieve a daily routine with a foster child, and who was proud of her success in getting him to sleep without trouble in his own room. She complained that when he went home to visit his mother she disrupted his routine, and slept with him in her bed. At the same time the mother complained that the foster mother was 'heartless' and made him sleep alone and friendless, fed him when it suited her, and forced him to use a potty to save her washing. The strain between them became too great and the fostering broke down.

A child is often hostile to his black mother, whom he sees so infrequently and whose visits seem to be full of tension and upsetting to the whole household. The foster mother is encouraged by this to think that the child prefers her because she is a better mother, and that everything is simpler when they are left to themselves. So she may discourage the natural parents' visits, by saying that all is well, and that they need not bother to come. On their part, the parents—especially if they have a large fare to pay to visit the foster home, their child is hostile, and the foster mother not welcoming—find it an easy option to stay at home and hardly visit at all. Mr Appeah, a Ghanaian, looking back to this sort of situation said,

> I told her I wanted to see my son, but it was always inconvenient for some reason, and she assured me many times that he was quite healthy, happy and doing well at school.

He gave up trying to arrange a visit, and as a result did not see his son for over a year, by which time the boy was very resentful towards his father.

Occasionally a quite different pattern develops. Natural parents, hearing horrific stories of black children being neglected in private foster homes, become very alarmed and acutely suspicious. They strip the clothes off their baby and inspect him minutely for any mark or sign of neglect. They complain loudly if he does not seem to be gaining weight fast, and try to persuade the foster mother to give him larger, stronger feeds more often. This usually results in nothing but offence and resentment. One mother complained that the foster mother was not in when she telephoned. Could she be working and leaving the baby alone in the house? There is also a very common fear that if African parents warn the foster mother that they intend to take their child back, she will lose interest in him from that time, and begin to neglect him, or even harm him. There is an old story—well known to West Africans in Britain amongst whom 'foster home' stories circulate widely—of a foster mother who gassed herself and her three foster children when she heard that they were to leave her for good. Many of the cases of children being suddenly removed from foster homes can be explained by the parents' fear of this happening to their child.

**Possessiveness**

The possessive foster mother is a phenomenon which the African parent finds hard to understand. 'Does she not know who are the child's parents?' 'Does she not remember who brought the child to her?' 'Who carried him for nine months before he was born?' 'Who does he look like?' are all questions asked by the incredulous parents. Multiple mothering is so much an accepted part of child-rearing in West Africa that the sharing concept is taken for granted, although the biological parentage of the child is never forgotten. In contrast to this the British foster mother belongs to a society which provides for legal adoption, and accepts that the long-term care of a child can provide a basis for a claim to keep him.

One West African student whose wife had died and who could not care for his child, signed adoption papers under the misapprehension that he was agreeing to some formal kind of fostering. He finished his studies and returned home. Four years later he returned to the local authority where the adoption had been arranged. He said, 'I have a good job at home now, and a new wife, who is very pleased to look after my son, and I have come to ask for him back.' He could not believe that he had unwittingly given up his child for ever to strangers, and could not even see him.

Adamson writes:[6]

> There were two highly significant variables to do with fostering and possessiveness; these were (a) the length of time the foster child had been in the foster home and (b) the frequency or infrequency of his contacts with his own parents during that time. These two findings . . . were proved beyond doubt to be most important factors in the fostering situation. The third variable significantly related to possessiveness was the foster parents having no child of their own.

Many foster mothers are lonely people whose only company is that of their foster child, but they would be shocked if they heard themselves described as 'possessive'. Sometimes it is the most rewarding relationship which they have ever had. Certainly they are conscious of a great investment of their time, money and emotions in the child. They are genuinely concerned for his future, but foresee it as a happier one if it could be spent with them. They often see it as their duty to protect the child from the threat of removal by his natural parents. Gradually, in contrast to the settled life he leads with them, a future with African parents becomes a terrifying prospect to child and foster parents alike. The parents are seen as frightening people with barbaric ways, who may at any moment disrupt the life of the child and the foster family by claiming his allegiance, or even 'kidnapping' him. Very often the whole situation becomes overlaid with racial prejudice. The parents' blackness, unusual social habits, and sometimes alarming manner are much discussed in front of the child, so that he too becomes racially prejudiced, confused and fearful.

Sula Wolff discusses the problems of foster children who need to have their parents' behaviour explained, 'so that they can eventually come to terms with it without having to think of their parents as "bad". Every child incorporates his parents; to some degree he *is* his mother and his father. To the extent that his parents seem "bad" to him, he himself feels bad and unlovable.'[7]

### A child's black identity

In caring for a black child, the white foster mother has an extremely difficult task. As Jane Rowe says in *Children Who Wait*: 'Parenting involves more than loving, more than providing food and shelter. Parents have a role as educators, standard setters, and disciplinarians' but, 'Relationships just do not stand still, and young children inevitably come to regard those who care for them as their parents.'[8] This is all very relevant to the black foster child. He is aspiring to the standards and example of white parents with whom he cannot entirely identify. He is often in a rural area, where all figures of authority and importance—teachers, doctors, health visitors, policemen, social workers and clergymen—are almost certain to be white. The black child growing up in this totally white community is at a loss for anyone who looks like him to enhance his self-image. One foster child said that he thought, although there were black and white children, everyone became white when grown-up. At seven years old, he was waiting to see a change in his colour.

In the official publication *Foster Care—A Guide to Practice* it is stated:[9]

> A black child growing up in an English home suffers a loss of culture, and when placed on a long-term basis he is eventually faced with identity problems related to his race and colour, and to his acquired values and attitudes.

This certainly is true of the black child in a private foster home. For the older child what Milner has to say about black identity and mental health seems particularly relevant:[10]

> The inferior image of his race makes for difficulties in identification with a despised and rejected group. He may identify with his own group, but then it is difficult to escape the implications of their derogatory identity for his own self-image. Alternatively he may identify with whites, which denies his true identity, is unrealistic, and fraught with anxiety. The problem presents itself as a choice between two evils. He may resolve it in one direction or the other, or he may stay in conflict over his identity; in each case he suffers anxiety and lowered self-esteem.

This is clearly the foster child's problem: part of him belongs to his white foster home, and yet he can never be a full member of it; part of him belongs to his African family, but he knows and understands very little of it. Most of these children opt for denying their blackness, but the stress and anxiety in that course are manifest in the tension with which they discuss it. Tunde is a teenage boy in a foster home who totally rejects his African identity. 'Why can't people leave me alone?', he says, 'I am English. I want to be English, not Nigerian. I don't want to know anything about Nigeria.' If that boy could be granted one wish, it would be to be white and a natural member of his foster family. And yet, because he is black, he is constantly the object of questioning by his peers: who are his parents? where do they come from? why has he never been to Nigeria? Grace is a Ghanaian girl of twelve who lives in constant fear of black people. Her foster mother has so persuaded her of their viciousness that she fears being snatched by any black strangers to be taken unwillingly to London, or worse still, Ghana, to live with her parents. She is genuinely afraid of all people who resemble her at all. Yinka, a Nigerian girl in a foster home in a market town in Kent, grew happily until she found that, when her friends were beginning to attract boys, none asked her out. She thought of all sorts of personal inadequacies as being the reasons, before she realised that it was because she was black. She suddenly became very race conscious, and suffered a serious depression, needing psychiatric treatment.

**Custody disputes**

In many cases children are left in foster homes unvisited and apparently abandoned by natural parents whose courage has failed them in the face of a hostile child and possessive foster parents. The situation continues fairly calmly for some time. The foster parents, even if they are receiving very small maintenance payments, make no complaint for fear of the child being removed; and the parents, although anxious, are often too unsure of their rights even to seek access to the child. The foster mother believing that she is protecting the child from parents he fears or dislikes, openly prevents the parents from entering the house. It is only when either the parents make some attempt to claim their child, or the foster parents ask for custody from a court in order to obtain legal sanction for their position, that the situation comes to a crisis.

When asked in a court case, with whom would he rather live, any child naturally says that he would prefer the home he knows to the uncertainty of one which may have been described to him as inadequate, and about which he can only speculate. Especially if there is a possibility of his family returning to Africa, the fears of such a child can be very real: the picture painted in the media, and often reinforced by an ignorant or malicious foster mother, of a wild continent full of fierce animals, snakes, magic and savagery cannot be a reassuring one for a young child. The fact that he might be going to an urban environment with his parents, or to warm, loving and welcoming relatives is not something he can picture and feel enthusiastic about.

The question of the child's identity—racial and cultural—is one of immense importance in these cases, but one which is often lost in a wave of sympathy (frequently fanned by ill-informed press reports), for the devoted foster mother who has done so much for so little, and who is to be deprived of the child she loves. In a recent case, a child of four years old was returned to his mother to go back with her to Africa, although he had not known her until six months before the decision of the court. A series of family crises had kept her out of

Britain, and prevented her from caring for him or even seeing him. During that six months before the court decision, she went to live near his foster home and during visits attempted to get to know him. She had little encouragement from the foster mother, but she was nevertheless able to build up a relationship with him, although he clearly still saw himself as a member of his foster family. The deciding issue was that his African identity and cultural heritage should not be denied him, and the judge awarded him to his own mother, who travelled back with him immediately to West Africa. There have been several cases, however, where older children have been awarded to their foster parents in a dispute, with only access given to their natural parents, because the children were considered to be too old to be transferred unwillingly to a new environment. In all cases, though, judges have tried to make the foster parents aware that the child has a real need to know his parents and to have an understanding of their culture, so that should he wish, he can at some future date renew his relationship with them, or assume his African identity.

However, when African parents are granted access to their children in foster homes, there are immense difficulties ahead, should the foster parents be hostile and unco-operative. The situation is similar to that of a parent seeking access to a child in the other parent's home after a divorce. The atmosphere in the home may be very unwelcoming, and the child not only feels resentful about the visit, disturbing as it does the tenor of his own life, but he often has strong guilt feelings at being the cause of unpleasantness and tension in the home he is anxious to regard as his own. He may even fear rejection by his foster parents if the access results in too many upsetting experiences for the family. Many children, by declaring that they do not wish to see their parents, hope that the problem (and their parents) will go away, and allow them to live a more peaceful life. They blame their parents for rejecting them in the first place, for placing them in the foster home, and now for making their lives difficult and tense by claiming them back. Older children sometimes avoid the access visits of their parents by leaving the house, or by refusing to speak to them, or even by developing functional illnesses when visits are expected. The access awarded by the court may be impossible for the parents to enjoy, and thus they are not able to establish a relationship with their children at all. They certainly cannot help them to come to terms with their black identity, or to understand their African culture.

### The return to Africa

When foster children return to Africa after many years in British foster homes, they often leave behind anguished and grieving foster parents, who anxiously follow news reports about Africa, write frantic letters to the children, the press, their MPs—anyone who will listen—trying to obtain information about the well-being of the children whom they have loved and cared for. These produce very little response, and they feel aggrieved and let down. But, as we have seen, the source of this sorrow can be traced to the initial misunderstandings when the foster placement began, many years before.

For their part, most African parents say that they have no intention of keeping alive a happy memory of the child's foster home. Mistakenly they believe that this would slow down the process of adjustment to African family life, and they fail to understand that internalized grief may cause greater emotional damage than if it is allowed free expression. They maintain that the child will yearn for his foster mother if he is reminded of her, but that if she is not mentioned, he will forget. They often even go to the extreme lengths of defaming her character, hoping that their child will turn against her memory, and all the more willingly embrace the new way of life with them. One can only imagine the anxieties and tensions which this creates. Many older children who have had this experience, become desperate to communicate with the family they have left behind, and will secretly smuggle out letters, and even try to save up a fare to return. Foster parents are naturally alarmed to receive unhappy letters in which the child complains bitterly about being homesick, the strange food, the unbearable heat, and what seems to him a bizarre way of life. Certainly he may be homesick and unhappy, but he will get used to some things like the food and the heat, and others can often be explained. One boy wrote that he was kept behind bars; the foster mother could not know that it is normal in most houses in the cities to have bars at the windows—to prevent burglars getting in, not to prevent children getting out! As a response to these letters, some foster parents send money, but this may not be very well received by the child's relatives; sometimes foster mothers send expensive presents to comfort the child, but these may not be given to him for his own, but just absorbed into the family. This can cause great unhappiness to a child who has been encouraged to treasure personal possessions.

Most children, however, adapt remarkably well, and many of the fears and anxieties of both foster mothers and social workers are unnecessary. The child discovers that he is part of a vast network of relations, who all take a warm personal interest in him, and this helps to compensate for the loss of the foster family. Western food is readily available, even in many of the villages, and a wise mother will ease her child gradually into an African diet. Many of the children, and indeed the parents, are ill during the first few months after their return home, but doctors say that a great deal of the illness could be prevented if parents realized that their children arriving from Europe have none of the immunity to tropical diseases of children born and reared in Africa. Malaria and dysentery are the biggest problems, but malaria can be avoided by the use of prophylactics, and dysentery by special precautions being taken in the preparation of food, and careful supervision of the child's diet, at least in the first few weeks.

A great many children, when they return to West Africa, are sent to one of the fee-paying international schools, where all the teaching is in English, and in which there are often a number of children from different countries. These schools are quite used to children from British schools, and understand that they may be behind in arithmetic, spell badly, and be poor at memory work; but they will express themselves well in English and show great initiative and curiosity. African education tends to be very traditional, and children are expected to work very hard and they have little opportunity for drawing and painting and may be discouraged from asking questions. The children from Britain are usually totally ignorant of the geography and history of Africa. However, most children do not feel unduly strange and isolated because, at least in the international schools, there will be many other children in the school who have lived in Britain and had similar experiences, and difficulties in adaptation.

At home, children soon learn to conform to the expected standards of behaviour, and very quickly accept their place in a more formal society. In a sense its very formality makes it easier for them to learn what is expected of them, and the lack of emphasis on individuality, while presenting difficulties initially, helps them to be absorbed more quickly. The involvement of children in adult life is a positive demonstration of their being accepted as useful and integral members of the family. After two years in Accra, Comfort (a child from case history VI) was visited by a social worker who had known her in England. Comfort had been doing her personal washing, and was walking across the compound with a basin of clothes on her head, 'not quite as effortlessly as most girls would have carried it', commented the social worker, 'but certainly with a competence and grace that would be rare in England.' Comfort was by then attending one of the best schools in the country, so there was no question of her being degraded and made to work as a poor relation. She had simply adapted to the way that girls of her own age behaved. On another occasion she was carrying a young baby on her back, proud that she was taking responsibility for her little cousin, and looking very unlike someone who had been brought up in Britain.

Some children return with their parents to Africa with happy memories and a continuing contact with their foster parents. Regular correspondence is maintained, and photographs and presents exchanged. In the African home, photographs of the foster family are displayed, and the children encouraged to remember the names of all its members. Nevertheless, it is probable that most children feel immense relief when they go to live in Africa with their parents, even if they have been born in Britain. They recognize that they are just like everyone else. They may never have experienced racial prejudice in Britain, but there is tension in being different and conspicuous, and this tension is often underestimated by foster mothers and social workers who have never experienced it, being members of the majority group. Without doubt, a child who has been happily fostered will adapt more easily to the new life than an insecure and disturbed child. However, it eases any child's anxieties if he is prepared for his journey to Africa by a positive attitude towards his home and culture, and the acceptance from the outset that he will return to it. These things are more important than the actual information he is given, but with an older child some knowledge can help to prepare him, and allay his fears of the unknown.[11]

A minority of West African children remain in their British foster homes until adulthood, but even they need to know something of their origins, and should be encouraged to find out about their own history and culture, and, although they live in Britain, to be proud of their African heritage. Many of them, as young adults, wish to search out their African identity, and they find to their astonishment, that they are not prepared for life in Africa. They are simply not able to adjust to the way of life or to the extended family, who find them strangely alien and unacceptable. In one tragic case, a girl who felt she no longer could live in a racist Britain, travelled to West Africa and searched out her relations. Sadly, she could not understand their ways and they could not understand her. She did not feel at home in Africa any more than in Britain, and in despair, she killed herself.

## Conclusion

Placing children in foster homes is not a happy solution for most families. Even in those arrangements which work tolerably well, the children eventually have to make major adjustments, which can cause great distress and are often damaging. When things go wrong, and there is conflict, the victims are the confused and bewildered children, whose loyalties are divided, whose identity is blurred, and whose mental health is endangered.

Social workers supervising the private placement of West African children in foster homes may find the following vital points useful to bear in mind:

(a) West African children are never up for adoption;
(b) Parents will certainly want their children home sooner or later;
(c) Foster parents should be encouraged to welcome visits from the children's parents;
(d) Children will be snatched if foster mothers are not encouraged to realize that the children's return to their parents is inevitable;
(e) Children should be prepared for a return to Africa;
(f) Most West African parents if approached sympathetically are very glad to work with social workers for the good of their children.

## Notes

1 R. Holman, *Trading in Children,* Routledge & Kegan Paul, 1973, p. 261.

2 Ibid., p. 68.

3 Personal communication.

4 A. McWhinnie, 'The Role of the Social Services', Commonwealth Students' Children Society, report of seminar on the African child in Great Britain, 1975, p. 25.

5 H. Ware, 'The Changing African Family in West Africa', in ibid., p. 9.

6 G. Adamson, *The Care-Takers,* Bookstall Publications, 1973, p. 191.

7 S. Wolff, *Children Under Stress,* Harmondsworth, Penguin Books, 1973, pp. 250-1.

8 J. Rowe and L. Lambert, *Children Who Wait,* Association of British Adoption Agencies, 1973, p. 104.

9 *Foster Care—A Guide to Practice,* HMSO, 1976, p. 43.

10 D. Milner, *Children and Race,* Harmondsworth, Penguin Books, 1975, p. 146.

11 A list of suitable children's books is to be found on pages 134-5.

Chapter Six

# British law and the West African child

*June Ellis*

The Welfare of a child is indivisible

(The Children Act, 1948)

In this chapter the legal framework of local authority fostering and of private fostering will be examined, and custody disputes involving West African children will be discussed. The status of custodianship, which was introduced in the 1975 Children Act and which has implications for West African children and their parents, will be considered, along with the powers conferred by the Act on the Secretary of State to issue regulations to govern private fostering, though at the time of writing these are not yet implemented.

A majority of foster children are placed in foster homes by the local authority; the remainder, formerly known as 'child protection' cases, are private foster children who are placed by their parents or guardians, and West African children fall almost entirely into this category.

Whether fostering is done through the local authority, or privately, it is always a temporary state. It may involve the care of a child, for many years, by adults who are not his parents but the legal ties with the natural parents remain.

## Child care legislation

The 1948 Children Act is the major enabling legislation relating to local authority fostering. It followed the report, in 1946, of the Curtis Committee which had been set up, as a result of the tragic death of a foster child, to enquire into the whole question of child care services in England. The Curtis Committee made many criticisms of the child care system and the Children Act of 1948 implemented its main recommendations, some of which will be considered.

## Receiving children into care

The Act widened the powers and responsibilities of the local authority in relation to taking children into public care, and made it simpler and quicker for action to be taken when children were in need. Whereas until this time, children could only be taken into care as a result of court proceedings, the Act placed a duty on local authorities to receive children into care without court proceedings, where the parents were unable to look after their children or prevented from doing so, and where it was in the interests of the child that this should be done. Part I Section I

A child may be admitted into care if it can be shown

(a) that he has neither parent nor guardian or has been and remains abandoned by his parents or guardians or is lost; or
(b) that his parents or guardian are, for the time being or permanently, prevented by reason of mental or bodily disease or infirmity or other incapacity or any other circumstances from providing for his proper accommodation, maintenance and upbringing; and
(c) in either case, that the intervention of the local authority under this section is necessary in the interests or the welfare of the child.

There is a duty to return the child to his parents as soon as it is in his interests. Part I Section 3

## Treatment of children in care

Detailed provisions were made for the care of children who were the responsibility of the local authority. A general duty was placed on the local authority 'to exercise their powers with respect to (a child in their care) so as to further his best interests, and to afford him opportunity for the proper development of his character and abilities.' It was recognized that fostering was likely to provide the best possible alternative for those children who were deprived of a normal home life, and so wherever possible local authorities were to 'board out', that is to foster, children in their care unless 'not practicable or desirable for the time being'. Part II

## The fostering of children by the local authority

In the 1948 Act the Secretary of State was given power to issue regulations to govern fostering, and seven years later in 1955 the Boarding-Out of Children Regulations were published. It is to be emphasized that these do not apply to privately fostered children, but only to those who are in the care of the local authority and placed in foster homes by them. The Regulations, which are still in effect, are detailed, precise, and comprehensive, numbering thirty-five in all. Some of the more important requirements are as follows:

*Selection of foster parents*

A child can only be boarded-out with a married couple or a single
Regulation 2 woman or—where he is boarded-out with a man—this must be a
grandfather, uncle or elder brother. Where long-term fostering is
envisaged, the foster child shall, wherever possible, be boarded-out
Regulation 19 with foster parents who are of the same religion as the child or who
undertake to bring him up in this religion. In addition, placements
are to be in homes that have been selected, or approved, by the local
authority. Before a child is placed, the home must be visited by a
Regulation 17 social worker, who is required to make a written report, showing
that it is suitable for the needs of that particular child.

*Duties of foster parents*

Regulation 20 and Schedule to Regulations Foster parents are required to sign a form giving specific undertakings: for example to bring up the foster child as though he were their own, to allow visits from the social worker, and to agree to the child being removed from the foster home if the local authority requests this.

*Visiting*

Regulation 21 The child and the home must be visited by a social worker within one month of the start of the placement. Afterwards, children under five are to be visited at least every six weeks for the first two years, and once every three months afterwards. A child who is more than five at the time of the placement, must be visited every two months for the first two years, and then every three months. In addition, the social worker is required to visit the foster home, or see the child, within one month of any change of address, and immediately, if there is any complaint about the child or made by the child himself.

*Reports*

Regulation 9 The social worker must make a written report after each visit to a
foster home, taking account of such factors as the welfare of the
child and the condition of the foster home. In addition, reviews of
the child's progress are to be made three months after the start of
Regulation 22 the placement, and at least every six months subsequently, by
someone other than the visiting social worker.

*Removal*

Regulation 4

The local authority has the power to remove any child in its care from any foster home, where it considers that the placement is no longer in the child's best interests.

The local authority, therefore, in discharging its duties towards children it places in foster homes, is given quite specific guidance as to what these duties are.

## Private fostering

It will be recognized that West African children normally come outside the local authority's terms of reference: they have parents; they have not been abandoned; the parents could—if they chose—give a lower priority to their studies and look after their children themselves. If West African parents wish their children to be fostered, they must arrange this themselves and private fostering, as will be seen, has many fewer safeguards for the children than local authority fostering.

Part V
Section 35

The Curtis Committee had made only brief reference to 'child protection' children in their Report, and the 1948 Act, which was concerned primarily with children 'in care', also had little to say about them. It simply re-stated the provisions of the Public Health Act of 1936 which had 'required foster parents to notify welfare authorities of the receipt of foster children and of removal or death', and had provided 'for the appointment of child protection visitors, and for the removal, upon the application by a welfare or local authority to a court of summary jurisdiction of children from unsuitable foster parents or premises'. There were two departures, however, and the 1948 Act extended these provisions, which had only applied to children under nine, to include those over nine but of compulsory school age, and the duty to supervise passed from the health authorities to the new child care service.

It was recognized that there was a need to re-state and clarify the position in relation to private fostering, but it was not until 1958 that there was a Children Act in which private fostering was specifically considered. It sought to provide adequate safeguards for the well-being of private foster children, and to ensure a system of supervision that could be administered simply and effectively by local authorities. Although there was virtually nothing new in the revision, local authority powers in relation to private fostering were strengthened. The most important sections are as follows:

*General duty of the authority*

Part I

Local authorities are required to visit private foster children within their area 'from time to time' and 'satisfy themselves as to the well-being of the children and give such advice as to their care and maintenance as may appear to be needed'.

*Duty of private foster parents to notify the local authority*

Part I Section 3 Anyone intending to take a foster child must notify the local authority at least two weeks beforehand; (previously, only seven days' notice had been required) and, in any case, no more than one week afterwards. Similar notifications are to be given when a foster parent changes address. Where a foster child is removed from a foster home the foster parent has to notify the local authority within forty-eight hours, giving the address to which the child has gone, where possible.

*Information that may be requested from private foster parents*

Part I Section 3 The local authority may require the foster parents to give the name, sex, date and place of birth of the child they are fostering, or proposing to foster, along with the name and address of the child's parents or guardian.

*Powers to prohibit placements*

The local authority's powers of prohibition are of two sorts. First, they relate to persons. Those who are disqualified from keeping a
Part I Section 6 foster child, unless the authority gives its consent, are persons who have had a child removed from their care either under the 1958 Act or under the 1933 Children and Young Persons Act; persons who have been convicted of any offence specified in the First Schedule of the 1933 Children and Young Persons Act; persons who have lost their parental rights under Section Two of the 1948 Children Act; persons who have been refused registration as a child-minder under the Nurseries and Child-Minders Act 1948, or whose registration has been cancelled. Second, the local authority may prohibit the making of placements where they are dissatisfied with the premises: 'Where
Part I Section 4 a person proposes to keep a foster child in any premises and the local authority are of the opinion that it would be detrimental to that child to be kept . . . in those premises, the local authority may prohibit him from doing so.'

*Powers to remove private foster children*

If a local authority wishes to have a child removed from a private
Part I Section 7 foster home, an application must be made to a juvenile court for his removal, on the grounds that the foster parent is unfit to have the

care of the child; has been disqualified from receiving a child for one of the reasons given in Part I, Section 4 or Section 6 of the Act; or that the child is being kept 'in any premises or any environment detrimental or likely to be detrimental to him'. As with the local authority's powers to prohibit placements, there is a right of appeal to the court.

The 1958 Children Act, with minor amendments introduced by the 1969 Children and Young Persons Act, remained the effective legislation until 1975. The 1969 Act had made it clear, as the 1958 Act had not, that unsuitability of premises was an adequate ground (Part II Section 55) for prohibition of private fostering placements, and this was a welcome clarification. Further, it extended the definition of private foster children to include those for whom 'reward' that is, 'payment (Part II Section 52) in cash or kind' is not made. Further, instead of visiting 'from time to time' as they were 'enjoined' to do by the 1958 Act, local authorities were to visit from time to time, as 'appropriate': a change (Part II Section 51) which, if anything, made visiting even more discretionary. But the 1969 Act, by requiring notification of placements to be made only in respect of a general intention to foster, and not in relation to each child, and when ceasing to foster altogether rather than when each (Part II Section 53) child moved, made the requirements less rigorous than before.

## Comparison of local authority fostering and private fostering

If these regulations are compared with those enumerated in relation to children fostered by the local authority, it is apparent that they are much less exacting. They are not so detailed or comprehensive and have less force. The social worker has no duty to visit the private foster child at stipulated intervals, and is given no specific directions in relation to these visits, nor required to make reports on them; in contrast, visits to children fostered by the local authority are particularized, written reports on these visits are mandatory and there is built-in provision for regular reviews of the fostering placement. The requirement to notify the local authority of a private placement, which is a prerequisite of control and supervision, is widely disregarded.[1] Although the local authority has powers in relation to prohibition of private placements, and removal of private foster children, these are cumbersome when compared with the direct powers invested in them in respect of local authority children, and they are seldom used.

Although it might be argued that there are adequate legal safeguards for privately placed foster children, in practice these are not effective. The discretionary nature of the regulations, and the limited powers of social workers, coupled with the *laissez-faire* approach to private fostering of local authorities, have led to a situation in which there are two levels of service provided, and these arise from the circumstances leading to fostering rather than from the children's needs.

## Custody disputes

Sometimes disputes arise over who should have the custody of a foster child, especially when the child has been in a foster home for a long time. The basic assumption in law is that fostering is temporary and that a parent or, in appropriate circumstances, a local authority is entitled to take a child back from a foster home. Thus, the Children Act, 1948, makes it clear that a child who is placed in the care of the local authority voluntarily by parents, can be taken back at any time by them. And the Boarding-Out Regulations of 1955 require that the foster parents shall agree to give up a foster child when they are required to do so by the local authority. Although the local authority may become involved in court cases, for instance where a foster parent resists an attempt to remove a foster child, legal disputes are more likely to arise in relation to privately fostered children where the situation is less circumscribed by law and regulation.

Part I Section 3

Regulations 5 and 20

The 'tug-of-love' cases that reach the courts, generally do so through an originating summons taken out by an anxious foster parent making the child a ward of court so that, pending court proceedings, he cannot be removed from the foster home. They could also arise as a result of equally anxious natural parents applying for a writ of *habeas corpus* to force an unwilling foster parent to give back the child, but this is rare.

A number of such disputes have involved West African children in British foster homes. One such case, Re O[2] (a minor) involved a Ghanaian girl, aged nine, who had lived with English foster parents since she was three months old. In December 1972 they applied to the Family Court for care and control. Quoting from the judgment will give a good indication of the complexity of the issues involved.

> The parents married in 1960, the husband came to England to study for a nursing certificate and the wife followed in 1961. The girl was born in 1963, a planned and wanted baby, but the parents had no plans for her. The foster-mother met the father when she was working as a nursing sister in the same hospital. The foster-parents realized that they could have no children of their own and were placed on the list of an adoption society as prospective adopters if a child became available. The natural parents both wanted to go out to work—the mother had qualified as a nurse—and their search for a child minder was unsuccessful.

> The natural father met the foster-mother in the street and explained his difficulty to her, and the girl had been with the foster parents ever since. The natural parents had had two more children, one of whom had spent some time with other foster parents.
>
> The natural parents had not made any contribution to her upkeep except occasional gifts of clothes and small amounts of money on two occasions. Up to 1970 they only visited the child about six times a year. During the last summer holidays she had stayed with her natural parents for some weeks but had become distressed at hearing of her proposed return to Ghana and had telephoned her foster-parents, who had collected her.

Wardship proceedings were started by the foster parents, and the child was made a ward of court. The hearing to decide care and control lasted eight days, and in reaching its decision the court was guided by the Guardianship of Minors Act 1971 which lays down that the welfare of the minor shall be 'the first and paramount consideration' in any case where custody is in dispute. This means that other considerations, such as ties of blood and the wishes of an unimpeachable parent may be taken into account, but the child's welfare is paramount. The President's summing up highlights the difficulties of deciding what is in the child's best interests.

He clearly placed great importance on psychological parenting, commenting with approval, on the 'loving care' the child received in the foster home, and describing the attachments she had formed there. He was influenced by the child herself:

> His Lordship had seen the girl. She was intelligent, talkative, cheerful, sociable, self-reliant and extrovert—a beautiful child who had put his Lordship at ease. She called her natural parents by their names, but the foster parents 'Mummy and Daddy'. She was well aware that the Official Solicitor was submitting that she should be returned to her own parents and she was determined that his Lordship should know her views. She sent him a long letter in which she stated quite categorically that she wanted to stay with her foster parents in England and not go to Ghana. The letter was written spontaneously without any indoctrination—unless it was the indoctrination of nine years of loving care.

On the other hand, the President was unimpressed by the natural parents:

> the parents had delegated all their responsibility for nine years and had told untruths about payments and contact with the child in an attempt to persuade the court of their fitness to

> have her. . . . The father had said that he could not go back to Ghana without the child because his family would think that he had sold or pawned her. He would lose face. [He] was incapable of realizing that it was fostering over nine years that had caused the trouble and had no real insight into the girl's standards, character and outlook.

In considering the long-term prospects, the President conceded that the child might confront prejudice later on, in Britain, but pointed out that she might face problems in Ghana, too, because of her Englishness: 'The girl could well be the butt of children in Accra because she spoke with an English accent and could not speak the language of her parents.' This seems to overlook the fact that language difficulties can be overcome, whereas colour remains, but the judge was in a difficult position in assessing alternatives, as no evidence was available about the conditions the child would return to in Ghana, and this was almost certainly significant for the decision to be reached: 'To go to Ghana was an irreversible and irretrievable decision . . . the girl should stay where she had always been, despite the blood tie, race and colour.'

The case was heard on appeal in February 1973,[3] and the appeal was dismissed. The three judges agreed that care and control should remain with the English foster parents. In giving judgment Lord Justice Davies considered evidence from a psychiatrist that it would be best for the child to return to Ghana with her parents, and that 'the short-term trauma of being separated from her foster parents would be much less serious than that which the child might later experience were she allowed to remain here, and that if she went to Ghana she would readily adjust to the change of circumstances.' He also quoted from an earlier case in re Thain ((1926) Ch. 676, 684) where Mr Justice Eve had said that although a little girl would be greatly distressed at parting from the couple with whom she had been living 'one knew from experience how mercifully transient were the effects of such parting and how soon the novelty of fresh surroundings and associations effaced the recollections of former days'. However, having weighed the evidence, he discounted it; 'the climate of opinion had changed'. His Lordship would fully accept Lord MacDermott's view in ((1970) AC 668, 715) (in the Spanish boy's case) that a change of custody might cause serious harm to young children. Referring to the psychiatrist's evidence, he again quoted from the Spanish boy's case to the effect that

> such evidence might be valuable . . . but only as an element to support the judge's general knowledge and experience, and a judge, in his discretion, should not hesitate to take risks, and go against the medical evidence if on a consideration of all the

> circumstances he considered that the paramount welfare of the infant, on the balance of probabilities, pointed to a particular course as being the proper one.

In conclusion, Lord Justice Davies agreed with the judgment in the lower court, in Re O,

> that save for blood and colour, she was wholly English. If she were taken away, she might, quite apart from unhappiness and homesickness, suffer both in the long and short view an emotional trauma which might well affect her for life . . . everything pointed to maintaining the status quo. If the child remained, there was no reason to anticipate that anything would go wrong. She would remain in all probability an ordinary English girl, save for her colour. And there were more and more English children in this country who were coloured. But in Ghana, quite apart from the inevitable heartbreak, it was not possible to forecast with any certainty what the future would hold.

In a similar case, heard more recently, Mr Justice Latey again emphasized the child's experiences rather than blood relationships and parental rights. In commenting, in open court, on his decision that the three children of a former African minister and his barrister wife should remain with their English foster parents of modest background, with whom they had spent many years, he said, 'You can remove a seedling that has scarcely begun to grow its roots and plant it elsewhere with perhaps little risk of harm. Seldom so with a young tree where the roots have grown deep in one kind of soil.'[4] Most people in Britain would probably agree with this view, though the problem may be in deciding when a seedling becomes a young tree.

These cases reflect changing attitudes towards parental rights, and the rights of children, for in case law there has long been an unequivocal emphasis on the rights of biological parents, and as recently as 1966 in Re C (M.A.) 1 All ER 838 the 'blood-tie' case, the judges referred to a baby's instinctual bond with his biological father, who was unknown to him, and the advantages of being brought up by his 'own people'; and in Re W (1970) QB 589, in upholding as not unreasonable a mother's refusal to give consent to her child being adopted, judges spoke of the 'bond between mother and child' being 'the strongest that nature forges'.[5] But the climate of opinion is changing fast, and is now one in which greater attention is paid to the child's own views and experiences, in considering matters of welfare.[6]

## The 1975 Children Act

The 1975 Children Act is the first major piece of legislation concerned with fostering since 1958. It is designed to safeguard and promote the child's best interests by providing a range of alternatives for those without a satisfactory home life and deals with adoption, fostering, custody and children in care. The sections that are especially relevant to West African foster children are related to custodianship, and to the powers given to the Secretary of State to introduce regulations to govern advertising and private fostering.

### *Custodianship*

Part II Section 33 Custodianship is a new status intoduced by the Act. It was recommended in the 1972 Houghton Report on adoption, although it was then termed 'guardianship', as a means of giving security to children who could not be adopted and of providing an alternative to the adoption of a child within the family and, in so far as it does this, it is to be welcomed. Custodianship is a status between fostering and adoption. By it, the natural parental rights and duties in respect of a child are suspended, and granted to an adult, other than his parents. The custodian can thus make day-to-day decisions concerning the child and these include matters relating to marriage, education and health. But the custodian does not have the right to arrange for a child's emigration, or to consent to his adoption, or to change the child's name. While the custodianship order is in force, the court may refuse access to the natural parents, and the custodian
Section 34 may apply to the court requiring payments towards the child's maintenance from his mother or father.[7] There is no automatic right of a local authority to supervise a child in respect of whom a custodianship order is granted. Either the natural parents, or the
Section 35 foster parents, may apply to have a custodianship order revoked.

Section 33 *Applications for custodianship* There are a number of grounds on which application for custodianship can be made, with the consent of the person who has legal custody. There is a further ground, which has an obvious relevance to long-term fostering arrangements, and which does not require the consent of the person having legal custody: an application for custody may be made by 'any person with whom the child has had his home for a period or periods before the making of the application which amount to at least three years and include the three months preceding the making of the application.'

The effect of such an application (where the applicant has
Section 41 provided a home for at least three years) is to freeze the situation:

before the hearing, no one is entitled to remove the child against the wishes of the applicant, without the court's consent.

*Custodianship disputes* In the event of disputes arising over custodianship, the Act makes it plain that the principle set down in the Guardianship of Minors Act 1971 will apply. The welfare of the minor shall be 'the first and paramount consideration'. Foster parents in a contested case, will have to show that it is in the child's interests to remain with them, and not necessarily that the natural parents are in some way deficient. Section 33

*Private fostering*

It was not originally intended that private fostering should have any place in the 1975 Bill, but disquiet on the part of those working in the field of private fostering led to changes during the committee stages, and three amendments relating to private fostering were introduced, though they have not at the time of writing been implemented. These are considered below.

*Advertising*

Advertising in the field of private foster care is a cause for some concern. The 1958 Act had prohibited the placing of anonymous advertisements. New subsections were inserted into the 1958 Act (Section 37) by the 1975 Act, enabling the Secretary of State to frame regulations to control advertising either by parents seeking foster homes for their children, or by prospective foster parents. Section 97

*Notification*

Those foster parents who have not, under existing legislation, informed the local authority that they are fostering, must do so within eight weeks of the publication of the regulations. The 1958 Children Act had required foster parents to notify the local authority of an intention to take a foster child. The 1975 Act inserts a section into the earlier Act (Section 3A) by which the Secretary of State may require similar notification by the natural parents of an intention to place a child in a foster home. Section 95 Section 96

> The Secretary of State may by regulations made by statutory instrument make provision for requiring parents whose children are or are going to be maintained as foster children to give to the local authority for the area where the children are, or are going to be, living as foster children, such information about the fostering as may be specified in the regulations.

*Supervision of placements* The requirement of the 1958 Children Act that a local authority officer should visit a private foster child 'from time to time' is amended to 'in accordance with the regulations made under section 2A of this Act': Section 2A reads, 'The Secretary of State may make regulations requiring foster children in a local Section 98 authority's area to be visited by an officer of the local authority on specified occasions or within specified periods of time.' It will be seen that this provides for the closer regulation of fostering on the lines already laid down for local authority children.

This control is much needed and it might well be argued that the 1975 Act itself, by strengthening the position of the foster parent, through the introduction of custodianship, makes the enlargement of statutory responsibilities in relation to private fostering, even more important than before.

## Notes

1 In his study of private fostering, Holman found that 94 per cent of the cases studied only came to the attention of the departments after the placement had started. In an unknown number of cases, of course, notification is never given. R. Holman, *Trading in Children,* Routledge & Kegan Paul, 1973, p. 222.

2 *The Times,* 'law report', 4 December 1972.

3 *The Times,* 'law report', 26 February 1973.

4 *Guardian,* 27 January 1977.

5 Referred to in M.D.A. Freeman, *The Children Act 1975. Text with Concise Commentary,* Sweet & Maxwell, 1976, introductory notes (no page reference).

6 See for instance J. Goldstein, A. Freud and A. J. Solnit, *Beyond the Best Interests of the Child,* Free Press, Collier-Macmillan, 1973, which has been influential in the movement towards a concern with children's rights.

7 Freeman, op. cit., p. 33.

Chapter Seven

# Conclusions

*June Ellis*

Against the view that we need to pay special attention to ethnic minorities, it is sometimes argued that to separate them out in any way from the host community is undesirable. It is true that general improvements in the social services and in income maintenance provisions would benefit ethnic minorities along with many others but, in addition to the many disadvantages they share with those who are part of the major culture, minorities have special difficulties that come from having left their own countries, from their different value systems, and from experiencing prejudice and discrimination.

More than fifty years ago in the USA, Mary Richmond emphasized the importance of taking account of the 'old world' backgrounds of social work clients who were immigrants to the 'new world' if such clients were to be effectively helped. Though we are working in a different time and other cultures are involved, what she said remains essentially true; it is equally important today that social workers in Britain should be aware of the cultural backgrounds of those who have come from overseas and to the social work implications of these differences.

However, in Britain, the movement towards more broadly-based social work, the increase in social science knowledge and the reorganization of social services departments, which have all provided new and exciting opportunities, have at the same time contributed to a tendency for particular 'client groups', among them ethnic minorities, to be overlooked. Whatever the reasons for this, and they are likely to be complex, social services departments and social work courses, with few exceptions, have yet to come to grips with the needs of those who have come to Britain from overseas.

Some agencies, recognizing that minority groups do have special needs, have responded by making well-meaning but misguided attempts to take account of these by assigning all 'coloured' clients to a 'coloured' worker. Clients and worker may have little in common, and such a practice reveals a disturbing lack of appreciation of the great cultural variety that exists outside of the British view of the world. We hope that in this book we have gone some way towards dispelling such a simplistic view by showing, for instance, that West Africans, though they may appear physically similar to West Indians to the European eye, differ in important ways from them.

However, the danger in emphasizing cultural factors, as we have done, is that almost everything may come to be seen in these terms, and the social worker who is concerned to be 'understanding' may be led, for instance, into the trap of supposing that behaviour that is indicative of psychosis is nothing more than a cultural manifestation.

There are profound difficulties here that cannot be resolved merely by reading a book. Therefore it is important that people with cross-cultural expertise should be available for the social worker to consult. Perhaps those authorities with responsibilities for significant numbers of West African children could consider the appointment of a worker (possibly a fostering liaison officer) who would have this kind of knowledge and understanding. The Commission for Racial Equality is a body which should also be able to provide consultative advice, and the Commonwealth Students' Children Society has been performing such a role for some years.

It is likely that West Africans will continue to come to Britain to study. This is to be welcomed, but we think that in many, if not in most, cases it is not in the interests of their children to be here. Our recommendations follow from the assumption that it is the welfare of these children that must be our prime concern, and the discussion that follows is guided by this belief.

Already, efforts are being made by the Commonwealth Students' Children Society to make intending students more aware of the difficulties they are likely to encounter should they come to Britain, and particularly the problems related to the care of their children. It is our view that students who already have children should be encouraged, if possible, to leave them at home in West Africa where there will usually be no difficulty in finding relatives willing to look after them.

The idea of advocating the separation of a child from his parents, for what may amount to a number of years, is only shocking in a British context. The earlier chapters have emphasized the relatively greater importance of the whole family in the lives of West Africans; the sense in which children belong to everyone; the way in which a child 'has many fathers and mothers' and so is related to his society at a number of points. It follows that remaining with the extended family, though separated from his biological parents, does not necessarily represent a deprivation. Furthermore, it could well be, because of the extent to which non-crisis kinship fostering is institutionalized in West Africa, that even if the child's parents themselves were at home the child would not be with them but would be staying with members of the family. The child whose parents are abroad, and who is staying with a relative, is thus not in any significant way different from many of his peers who are also being fostered within the extended family. He will be growing up as a full member of his society, with a security that comes from being part of the group, aware that his parents are not there but probably looking forward with some pride to their return as 'beentos'.

Some West Africans, of course, will wish to bring their children with them to Britain and, because of the importance of children to any West African marriage, many other West African children will be born here. The welfare of these children and their families would best be served if these children could live with their parents. For these families, better housing and improved day-care facilities would help in reducing the need to make use of private fostering; but to expect, at a time of economic stringency, that these deficiencies will be substantially remedied in the short term, is probably overhopeful. However, an indication of what may be achieved has been given by the Commonwealth Students' Children Society; they have formed a housing association and, with the help of the local authority, purchased the freeholds of houses and are making use of short-life property to house West African families with children. The Society's most ambitious scheme has been to convert a tenement block in East London into flats for fifty student families from the Commonwealth who agree to keep their children with them. There is a nursery school attached, and this has been equipped with the help of a grant from Ghana. We hope that ventures similar to this will continue to be mounted, possibly with financial aid from West Africa, and perhaps in conjunction with training institutions in this country; and some colleges and hospitals have already established nurseries for students' children.

These measures, unfortunately, touch only a few of the thousands of West African students in this country, and many will still make use of private fostering. This is likely, as is shown in Chapter five, to prove an unsatisfactory solution and we hope that, in the future, social workers who are approached by West African students for help in making fostering arrangements will take the opportunity to explore with these parents the possibility of returning their children to the extended family in West Africa. Clearly, if this is to be regarded as an option it requires great skill on the part of social workers if they are not to appear to be saying, 'We don't want your children.' It is also important that there should be social workers in

West Africa who are able to support and advise the families of these returned children. Exchange schemes for West African and British social workers would be important not only to increase understanding but also to build up lines of communication.

Despite efforts to encourage parents to avoid fostering, as long as West African students come to Britain, there are going to be substantial numbers of their children in British foster homes and it is essential that they should have greater safeguards than exist at present. This can be achieved in two ways: first, by legislative changes to improve the administrative framework of private fostering, and second, by increasing the expertise and cultural sensitivity of social workers who practise within this framework.

The question of amending the law in relation to private fostering raises important questions about parental rights, as well as posing problems in terms of social work resources, but against these have to be set considerations of children's welfare and the importance of preventing situations where children become objects of contention. We think that the need to safeguard the welfare of children (British as well as West African, though in this book we are especially concerned with the latter) justifies, indeed requires, an extension of statutory powers in relation to private fostering. We hope that the Secretary of State will use the powers conferred on him by the 1975 Children Act (see Chapter six) to regulate advertising by private individuals, as this would restrict the activities of some very unsuitable foster mothers. The powers given to him to require the natural parents as well as proposed foster parents to notify the intended placement of a child are welcomed. Knowing about placements is obviously a prerequisite of effective supervision but the notification rate has been very low. It is understandable that foster parents should not be very keen to notify placements to the local authority, perhaps feeling that they stand to lose rather than to gain in this (if they keep quiet perhaps they will be saved from 'interfering' social workers). It is very different with the natural parents however; Vivien Biggs has pointed out in Chapter five that they are generally very keen to work with social workers and certainly many approach social services departments for help over the care of their children and are disappointed when it is not provided. They would be likely to inform the social services department if they thought that by doing so they would be helping their children. Since communication amongst West Africans in Britain is good, it is probable that quite soon after such a regulation came into force there would be a reasonable level of notification which would increase as West Africans realized that others were being helped by social workers.

Given a shortage of foster parents it may not, in the short term, be possible to set up very stringent requirements in relation to their selection and approval; it is all the more important, therefore, that the supervision of these foster homes should be much more comprehensive than hitherto, and as exacting as for children who are placed by the authority after careful matching procedures. The enabling provision in the 1975 Act, requiring regular visits from a social worker at stipulated intervals would, if implemented, provide the kind of framework that would facilitate effective social work. In addition to clear-cut requirements for visiting by the local authority (which would go some way towards removing the ambiguity surrounding the social worker's role which has been inhibiting in the past), we recommend that there should be a duty placed on the social worker to work with the natural parents as well as the foster parents (this has not hitherto been the case), and that arrangements for liaising with workers in other authorities where the foster home and the parents are some distance apart, be carefully worked out. There should be the same requirements for the recording of visits and for reviewing the progress of the placement as with local authority fosterings.

It is essential that the placement should proceed in the full knowledge that the fostering arrangement is a temporary one, and that the aim is to reunite the child with his parents as soon as possible. Many placements that begin propitiously, with good will on both sides, end in acrimony because the temporary nature of the placement has been forgotten. The foster child settles down, becomes in many ways 'an English child', so that the suggestion that he should return to his own parents provokes hostility and resistance on the part of the foster parents and in many cases the child too. A number of the case histories at the end of the book illustrate this pattern.

Ideally, at the beginning of the placement there should be a meeting between all parties to draw up a written agreement so that it is clear from the outset what the expectations are: matters of payment ought to be discussed and agreed, and the importance of visiting often and maintaining contact with the child emphasized. In general, foster children who are able to maintain contact with their parents have been found to be better adjusted than those without such links, and for West African children, whose parents will certainly want them back, this contact, including regular holidays and weekends with the parents whenever possible, would seem to be especially important in forestalling the kind of tragic alienation illustrated in the case histories, and also in enabling all children to settle back with their parents more easily. It will be appreciated, in the light of what was said in Chapter three about attitudes to child-training, that the West African parent—not thinking in our psychological and developmental terms—may not easily understand the importance of such contact for the child and may shy away from visiting that is stressful for all concerned.

The ending of a placement may be as important for the child as its beginning. But foster parents commonly display a reluctance to face the possibility that the child will be going, and have genuinely little idea of what the child is to be prepared for; the real parents are also unlikely to appreciate the importance of such preparation, thinking that everything will be all right once the child is back home. An informed and sympathetic social worker can help the foster parent to accept the potential loss of a foster child, as part of an overall plan for the child, and can prepare the real parents to understand the behaviour difficulties that are likely to be encountered in a child who finds himself confronted with very different expectations and without the support of people on whom he has come to rely.

Many West African parents—and they are sometimes encouraged by foster parents—leave their children in foster homes longer than is necessary for what may seem to them to be good reasons: the foster parents' home in a rural environment appears much better than a cramped London flat, or the children seem settled in a particular school. Parents may even leave children in a foster home in Britain when they return to West Africa; they believe that it will be better if the children finish their education here. Arrangements such as these can become dangerously prolonged, with disastrous consequences, the child, all the while, becoming more and more 'English'.

Justified concern has been expressed about the effect on fostering of clause 33 in the 1975 Children Act. This enables foster parents to apply for custodianship against the wishes of parents after a child has been in a foster home for three years (see Chapter six). The new clause could have a disturbing effect on the fostering relationship: it might influence West African parents who are not very aware of the damaging effects of such an action to move a child from a foster home for no other reason than that the three years was almost up. It is also likely to encourage parents to keep plans to return to West Africa secret and then to remove their child without warning. Social work help is necessary here if parents are to feel secure enough not to move a child, who is otherwise satisfactorily placed, solely because of the danger of custodianship proceedings, and if the ending of the placement is to be planned for and worked towards.

The role of the social worker in trying to mediate, interpret and support is difficult and we have already expressed the hope that there will be sources of expert advice available to help them in working with West African clients. But, given that in Britian significant proportions of the population have different cultural backgrounds from those of the majority, many of them coming into the most disadvantaged sections of our society, it is important that serious attention should be given to the place of teaching about ethnic minority groups at basic training level and to ensuring that qualified social workers have an awareness of cultural variations and are alerted to the social work implications of these. Such an awareness, in relation to West Africans, might help to prevent some unnecessary admissions to care: for instance, a recognition that corporal punishment is used by most responsible West African parents to chastise a wayward child, and that the use of a stick or belt is common, might prevent precipitate action on the part of a social worker.

Concern has been expressed about the disproportionately large numbers of black children in care and especially residential care in Britain. Whilst the majority of these are West Indian, some are West African, and it is important that the efforts that are starting to be made to help young West Indians to develop a satisfying cultural identity should be paralleled by a similar concern in relation to West Africans in care. If there is no alternative to their remaining in care, every effort should be made to give them an understanding of what being a Yoruba or an Ewe means, and it is likely that West African organizations in Britain could be helpful here; for instance, West African student groups could give these children an idea of the richness of their own culture. Although efforts to recruit West African foster parents in Britain are unlikely to prove very successful, it may well be possible to engage the interest of West African volunteer workers in residential work and to increase the few West African social workers in this field so that children can relate to appropriate figures as they are growing up in a white world.

But there is another avenue that is promising for these children. For most of them there is a family somewhere in West Africa, perhaps unaware of where they are, perhaps under the misapprehension that they are getting some kind of superior boarding school education in Britain. If the alternative is growing up in care in Britain, it would seem well worth attempting to trace such families. The case history involving the three Ghanaian children, Comfort, Felix and Mabel, shows what can be accomplished in this direction. Although it involved some immediate expense and considerable work, it was less costly than supporting the children in care in Britain, and for those children the future looks brighter than it could have done here. It is important that a wish to avoid any suggestion of 'Powellism' should not blind people in Britain to the consideration of a return to Africa as a possibility. The question arises of course as to why the children are in care and this is something that would repay investigation. It would be important to discover whether their admission was associated with a full investigation of possible alternatives and whether, for instance, the father was contacted. If they came from a patrilineal tribe, he would certainly wish to take responsibility for the children. In the case history of Julian, the Ghanaian father was eager to take responsibility for his son, and the family was ready to accept the mixed race child without question. If this boy had not gone to Africa, he would, more than likely, soon have been in care with very little hope of a settled future.

In emphasizing the need to understand West African culture and in conveying respect for it, it is important not to underestimate the conflicts that can arise when different cultures meet. The emphasis in working with West Africans should be on preventing the kind of situation that arises when the child becomes an object of contention, for decisions such as those that have to be made in custody disputes there are no easy answers and it may well be, as the judge pointed out in Re O (Chapter six), that at this stage there is no right answer, only two wrong answers. However, even with better social work support, which we hope will make the issues and dangers clearer from the start, there are going to be disputes, some of them reaching the courts. There are many ongoing, long-term foster placements which have proceeded without social work help and with minimal parental involvement, thus the 1975 Act, which strengthens the hand of the foster parent, may well result in foster parents who have had West African foster children for a number of years deciding to apply for custodianship against the wishes of the African parents.

In Britain we readily acknowledge the importance of 'psychological parenting', and we are very sensitive to the distress suffered by a child who is removed from those he has come to regard as his parents. Increasingly, weight is given to the child's own views in matters concerning his welfare. These are all considerations that will favour a decision that a child who has been in a foster home for a number of years should stay with foster parents whom he knows and loves rather than be returned to parents who may be almost like strangers. And this may be right. We do not seek to deny the importance of such considerations but, because they are so widely accepted in our society, there is a need to ensure that we pay attention to other factors that are relevant but that may tend to be overlooked. Who can assess the trauma of a separation from those who have cared for a West African child, and whom he has come to regard as his parents, against the distress that possibly awaits such a child as a black adolescent in Britain? What seems to be a right decision at five or six may not appear so at fifteen or sixteen.

It would be wrong to suggest that no West African child could be happily integrated into a predominantly white Britain. This is clearly not so, and with understanding foster parents the chances may be good. But there are difficulties ahead that are to be set against the welcome that such a child is likely to be given on his return to his African family and the sense of relief, once there, from feeling that he is no longer different. It is worth quoting the views of a Nigerian girl, now at London University, who had been fostered all her life in an excellent home in a very friendly local community in Britain. She said that only when she stayed at an international hostel in London was she able to relax and no longer feel conspicuous. She added, 'I know I am a Nigerian but when I meet Nigerian students at university I don't know where I come from—I can't even say whether I am a Yoruba or an Ibo. I am glad I was never adopted, because I can never really belong here.'

Some foster parents will respond with tolerance and understanding to adolescent difficulties; others may not and feel that they cannot cope with a rebellious black teenager who seems so far removed from the attractive black toddler they took. It is by no means uncommon to meet a foster parent who dotes on a black foster child and yet, at the same time, evinces prejudice towards the child's parents and hostility towards his culture. Such ambivalent attitudes are bound to affect the black child who, in growing up, has to come to terms with his 'rejection' by his own parents, for that is how he may construe it, and with the rejection of part of him which is implied in the foster parents' attitudes to his own family.

Indeed, foster parent attitudes to West African society may be a significant factor to note in a custodianship dispute and an indication of possible troubles ahead. The important point here is that it would be perfectly simple for foster parents to apply for the custodianship order to be revoked; this can be done at any time. If this happens, the West African foster child might be in a dire situation. It might prove difficult to trace his own family, and at this age it would not be easy for a child to adjust to life in a different society. It is ironic—since the 1975 Children Act is concerned to increase the security of children in general—that its effect in relation to this particular group could be to decrease their security and to increase the number of disturbed black teenagers in care, and probably institutional care.

We should like to make the following recommendations in relation to custodianship disputes such as these involving two cultures. First, that those who are to make decisions about custodianship should be helped to understand the total situation. There should be a report to the courts from a social worker who has a close knowledge of the culture from which the child comes, as well as a report about the child's present circumstances. Probation officers, who generally make such reports, do not usually know much about West Africans and may not be especially expert in child care. Second, where custodianship is awarded to a private foster parent against the wishes of the natural parent, some form of social work supervision should be the rule rather than the exception (the court has the power to decide whether or not to require this). Such supervision would go a long way to ensure that legal rights of access are made effective. So often, as described in Chapter five and in the case histories, these rights have been difficult to implement. Third, in the event of such a custodianship order being revoked after the child's parents have left the country, every effort should be made to rehabilitate the child with his natural family in West Africa rather than leaving him to spend the rest of his childhood in care.

We have made recommendations which in our experience seem desirable and which afford greater safeguards for the West African child in Britain, but there is need for research so that more informed decisions can be made. There are provisions in the 1975 Children Act for the review of its workings, and it is hoped that the effects of the new status of custodianship will be carefully monitored so that in ten years' time we may know something about the 'success rate' in relation to custodianship orders. And there is need for longitudinal research on children returning to West Africa so that we can know more precisely the effects of moving from one society to another. The impression of social workers from the Commonwealth Students' Society, who have visited returned children in West Africa, is that many of the worst fears of foster parents in Britain are not realized and that the children settle down surprisingly well; but it must be remembered that a 'good' child, by West African standards—quiet, obedient and conforming—could also be a child who was secretly grieving. Perhaps we shall find out that the first five years of life are less important than has been thought and that later experiences and wider social influences have been undervalued in our society. Certainly research of this kind is likely to have an application beyond the specific concern that has been the focus of this book and could increase our understanding of socialization processes in general.

# Appendix: Case histories*

## I The Babalola family

Ade, a seven year old boy, was referred to a social worker because Mrs Smith, his foster mother in Hampshire, complained that his parents only paid her occasionally and rarely visited. His parents, Mr and Mrs Babalola who came from Nigeria, were living in London in one room of a multi-occupied house with their four younger boys, aged five, four, two and six months. There was little space in the damp and dingy room and Mr Babalola was obliged to take them to the park to avoid complaints of noise from other tenants.

Ade had been placed with Mr and Mrs Smith shortly after his birth owing to the serious illness of both parents. When they recovered, they visited Ade and were so pleased with his home in the country that they thought it would be wrong to bring him back to London in view of their difficult living conditions. They genuinely thought they were doing the best for their son and Mr and Mrs Smith appeared very understanding and told them to pay whenever they could manage it.

Within a short time Mrs Babalola became pregnant again and in spite of poor health produced four more children in rapid succession. It was difficult for her to make the journey to visit Ade with the young babies, so her husband went alone twice a year taking presents for Ade and the Smith family as he would have done at home. Mrs Babalola longed to see her son but the train fares for the whole family would have cost far too much.

When the social worker met the family, she immediately attempted to find better accommodation for them in preparation for Ade's return, and managed to raise funds for the whole family to visit Ade.

Ade was taken aback when his quiet country life was invaded by

*To preserve anonymity names, nationalities and place names have been altered.

his four younger brothers. They were skinny and spoke English with a funny London accent, his mother was fat and did her hair in strange plaits. He definitely preferred his white Mummy to this strange woman. Mrs Babalola was upset by his reaction and thought she had better stay away but the social worker tried to encourage visiting and also to persuade the Smiths that this was necessary however disturbing they found it. The Babalolas were worried because Ade seemed so estranged and wanted to bring him home immediately. They were persuaded by the social worker that this must be a gradual process and they must get to know him first. This seemed difficult in the strained atmosphere of the Smiths' home so they asked if he could come up to London for the day. Mrs Smith agreed only on condition that she stayed with him all the time. This she did and the parents again found it difficult to get near their son. He was critical of their living conditions, even though they had now been rehoused in spacious but low standard accommodation. There was only lino on the floor, no carpets, and hardly any toys.

Next time a visit was suggested Ade refused. Mrs Smith kept saying, 'He is an English boy now, he cannot go and live with those people, eating all that strange food.' Relationships seemed to deteriorate and the hoped-for gradual process of getting to know each other seemed doomed. The Babalolas were convinced that if only Ade were home with his brothers he would get on well with them and settle down. They felt the Smiths were poisoning his feelings. It was finally agreed that Ade should be collected and brought home at the end of the summer term. When the appointed day came, Mr Babalola went to the Smiths accompanied by a social worker to find the house was blocked by press men and angry neighbours all sympathizing with the foster parents. After a near hysterical scene which lasted about two hours inside the house, Ade was persuaded to walk to the car with his father and at least the photographers were thwarted in their hopes of seeing a physical struggle take place.

Ade who was now nearly nine, seemed to settle down amazingly quickly and by the end of the summer holidays had lost his Hampshire accent and spoke just like his brothers. His parents tried to make up to him for all he was missing by buying expensive toys, including a beautiful Chopper bicycle. But he was clearly a very confused little boy and found the strict way his parents disciplined him very strange after all the fuss made of him by the Smiths. In school too there was a very free atmosphere and the children were encouraged to express themselves, but at home it was a question of homework and housework and, as the eldest, Ade was naturally expected to be responsible for his siblings.

Mrs Babalola was doing an evening cleaning job to earn some

extra money and sometimes she left home before Mr Babalola came back from work, although usually it was not more than half an hour. During this time Ade was in charge of his four brothers and his baby sister now a few months old. One day his father came home and found Ade outside in the street riding up and down on his bicycle with the traffic whizzing by. Mr Babalola was angry, not only because Ade had broken the rule of never riding in the busy street, but because he had left the younger children alone in the house. He thrashed him with a belt so that he would remember the punishment and never disobey again.

Ade ran out of the house and two hours later was picked up by the police. He was taken into care on a 'place of safety order' and stayed in a children's home for a month. The Babalolas were confused and hurt—they loved their son and wanted him to grow up as a decent law-abiding citizen, but of course they had to chastise him if he was disobedient. The social worker understood their attitudes and after a month Ade was allowed to return home on a two years' supervision order. But the damage had been done. Ade was openly defiant and knew that his father could not cope with this situation. If he could not beat him what could he do to make him behave? The English people would not allow beating so Ade could do what he liked.

Throughout this period the question of the future of the family was frequently under discussion. Mrs Babalola confessed to the social worker that she hated life in England and wanted to go home. She was a very simple motherly woman, with no ambitions for herself, only for her children. She had never tried to pursue any studies but had concentrated on looking after the children and doing part-time jobs in the morning and evening when her husband was back home. Her health had been poor ever since she came to England and she felt confident that once she was home everything would be easier.

Mr Babalola was not so enthusiastic but raised as the main issue the impossibility of saving up enough money for their fares now that there were six children. He also queried how he could pay for the children's education in Nigeria. The real issues at stake became clear when the social worker came up with the possibility of funds being available and of contacts in Nigeria being willing to assist in job hunting if they could have photostats of Mr Babalola's qualifications. It then appeared that in fact he had not acquired any qualification of any kind—he was not working as a telecommunications engineer as he had led people to believe but as a cleaner. This was a terrible confession for Mr Babalola to have to make and his wife was deeply shocked. After ten years in England he had nothing to show but debts and of course six children! It seemed that all his hopes were now turned upon his children and he was determined that they should benefit from good schools in this country even if he had to be a cleaner all his life. The problems arising from Ade's behaviour now looked like destroying this ambition.

No one who saw them with their children could doubt that Mr and Mrs Babalola were devoted, caring parents who wanted to do the best they could for their children. By coming to Britain they had set in motion a whole series of negative events (there were many other serious difficulties, far too numerous to mention here). Failure meant it was impossible to return home. Economic necessity did not allow time for study even if there had been a realistic hope of achievement. If Mrs Babalola returned on her own, would her husband ever follow her? If they stayed here would their children be achievers or would they be swallowed up by the life style of the children in the area in which they were living where academic achievement was certainly not highly valued?

## II Mrs Uchende

Mrs Uchende came to England from Nigeria in 1961, aged thirty, to study nursing. She left her husband, a businessman, and three children behind and planned to return to them in 1965, when she obtained her SRN qualification.

During her time as a student nurse in Birmingham she became friendly with a Ghanaian doctor, by whom she became pregnant. Her daughter, Kate, was born in 1963 and, in order to continue her training, Mrs Uchende placed her privately with Mrs Harrison, a childless foster mother aged fifty-eight. She found Mrs Harrison through placing an advertisement in the *Nursery World*.

By 1967, Mrs Uchende had gained her SRN, and was anxious to return home with Kate. Mrs Harrison was heartbroken at being parted from her and Mrs Uchende says that she felt guilty at taking the child from her; but she finally did, with many promises to keep in touch and to let her know how Kate settled down.

In 1967 the Nigerian war broke out. Mrs Uchende and Kate were near Enugu, a part of the country much reported in England as 'war-torn'. Children were shown on television and in the press, orphaned and starving. Mrs Harrison became extremely agitated about Kate's safety and wrote anxious letters to Mrs Uchende every week, asking her to send Kate back to her, at least until the war was over. In 1968 Mr Harrison died and Mrs Harrison wrote more urgently, begging Mrs Uchende to send Kate to her, to keep her company, as she was now so lonely. Mrs Uchende and Kate had a difficult time during the war, moving about a good deal to avoid the fighting, and food was in short supply. They were, however, with a number of relatives who stayed together, and one of these, a teacher, gave Kate and her cousins lessons, and she is reported to have been very attentive and quick to learn.

In 1970, when the war was over, Mrs Uchende decided to come back to England to study midwifery and brought Kate with her. She was still in touch with Mrs Harrison, who urged her to let Kate come back to her. Mrs Uchende agreed to this and started her midwifery course in Birmingham, while Kate started school in Worcestershire.

As the months went by, Mrs Harrison dissuaded Mrs Uchende from visiting, reassuring her that Kate was well and happy. In 1971, after a gap of six months, Mrs Uchende visited one day to find both Mrs Harrison and Kate very hostile. Mrs Harrison said that she had heard from Kate about the terrible time she had had in Nigeria, and that she did not think she should see her mother, as it reminded her of the war and upset her. Kate was confused and tearful. Mrs Uchende was bewildered by this, but was deterred from visiting by Mrs Harrison, whom she telephoned each week. She was always told that Kate was well, but did not wish to see her.

Mrs Uchende finished her midwifery course in 1972, and asked to take Kate back to Nigeria with her. Mrs Harrison refused, and so Mrs Uchende got a job, nursing, in Birmingham, and began to visit Mrs Harrison and Kate more frequently, hoping to dispel all her frightening ideas about Nigeria and the war. However, when she visited, Kate was sulky and unresponsive, and Mrs Harrison openly abused Mrs Uchende in front of Kate. Kate started to fall behind her age-group in school, and developed a stammer. Mrs Harrison maintained that this was caused by Mrs Uchende's more frequent visits. Mrs Uchende became very anxious, but uncertain what to do. On one occasion in 1974, encouraged by some male relatives, she attempted to 'snatch' Kate, but the police were called, and they were told that they were trespassing and causing a nuisance. Kate was extremely upset by this incident.

In 1975 Mrs Harrison asked for custody of Kate from the court. This she was granted, with access for Mrs Uchende. Her attempts to use this access have never been successful, as Kate is openly hostile to her mother now and believes that she only wishes to have her because she will soon be of working age. She is a very disturbed girl of fourteen, with no settled racial identity; she says she wishes she was not black, that she hates her mother and that her home is with Mrs Harrison. She fears all black people, thinking that any one of them may be a relative, who will try to take her to Nigeria.

Mrs Harrison is now seventy-two, and has no relatives. Mrs Uchende is only in this country in order to keep in touch with Kate, although she is not succeeding. The rest of her children have grown up in Nigeria without her and her husband has taken another wife.

## III Julian

Julian, a Ghanaian, came to England in 1968, aged twenty to study law. He came from a highly educated well-to-do family in Accra, who were supporting him financially while he studied in London. In 1971 he formed a relationship with Jane, an English girl of his own age. She was attractive and vivacious but of very low intelligence and had left school at the age of fourteen. Her parents had not been able to control her and, since leaving school, she had lived an unsettled, promiscuous life. Her family were well known to the Birmingham social services department, as a family with multiple problems. Her father was an alcoholic, her brother was in prison, and her married sister's family were all under-achieving and truanting from school.

Jane found some stability in her relationship with Julian and they lived together in one room in West London. Jane became pregnant in 1972, and was anxious to have an abortion but Julian persuaded her to have the baby. A boy, Christopher, was born in October 1972. Julian and Jane quarrelled a great deal at the time of the baby's birth, as Jane was pressing him to get married.

Julian was reluctant to marry Jane, as he was nearing the end of his studies and planned to return to Ghana, where he knew that his family had arranged a suitable marriage partner for him. He was conscious of the fact that Jane, with her lack of education and low intelligence, would be a social handicap to him at home, and said that he thought she would be made to feel inferior and, therefore, the marriage would not work.

Julian was very fond of Christopher, did a great deal for him, and spoke very proudly of him as 'my son'. When he was preparing to return to Ghana, Julian and Jane quarrelled constantly, mostly about the future and, during one disagreement, Jane stabbed Julian with a knife. She frequently slept away from home and Julian cared for Christopher when she was not there.

In 1973 Julian returned to Ghana, leaving Jane with the baby in London, saying that he would send her money and offering to send fares to Ghana for both of them in 1974. Soon after he left, Jane discovered that she was pregnant again and claimed that Julian was the father. In correspondence with her, he always denied this. In early 1974, a baby girl was born, but died mysteriously when she was three weeks old. An open verdict was returned by the court. Jane started to neglect Christopher in favour of a colourful social life, with many boy friends, parties and outings. Christopher was taken into the care of the local authority.

At this point, Julian, in Ghana, became very anxious about his son and asked to have him. A home visit was arranged through the Social Welfare Department in Accra and it was found that Julian's mother and father, aged fifty and fifty-five, were prepared to have

Christopher until Julian was married. Julian's fiancée expressed her willingness to care for him when she was married. Jane, who had formed another relationship by this time, agreed that Christopher should go to his father.

And so it was arranged that Christopher should be taken by a social worker to Julian's sister, who was in London and who had agreed to escort him to Accra. This she did in October 1974. Christopher was two years old.

A report from a social worker in March 1975 said that Christopher was healthy and well settled in his new life. He had been given Julian's family surname and was much loved by many relatives. He attended a nursery school and seemed to be a happy, normal child for his age.

## IV The Thomas family

Mr and Mrs Thomas came to England from Sierra Leone in 1960, when both of them intended to study medicine. In 1962 Mary was born, and placed privately with Mrs Robertson a foster mother of forty-two in Sussex; in 1964 John was born and was sent to join Mary with Mrs Robertson; in 1967 Peter was born and also was placed with Mrs Robertson. The relationship between Mr and Mrs Thomas and the Robertson family was a very happy one. The Thomases visited every two or three weeks and Mr and Mrs Robertson welcomed them. The children were brought up in a very liberal way, encouraged to express themselves and had many educational toys. They went to a playgroup before school age and at five went to school locally in Sussex. Mr and Mrs Thomas lived in very cramped accommodation in London and never took the children with them to London; their contact was always in the Robertsons' home.

In 1968 Mr Thomas qualified as a doctor, and returned to Sierra Leone. Owing to the three breaks when the children were born, Mrs Thomas still had three years more to do to qualify. She continued to live in London and visit her family in Sussex. She was still paying £2.00 per week for each child to Mrs Robertson, which was the original sum agreed in 1962, but Mrs Robertson did not ask for any more and Mrs Thomas could not afford to offer it.

In 1971, Mrs Thomas also qualified as a doctor and told Mrs Robertson that when she had packed up, she would collect the children and take them with her to Sierra Leone, where Dr Thomas, her husband, now had a home waiting for them. To her surprise, Mrs Robertson said that she could not uproot the children from the life they were used to and insisted that they be allowed to finish their schooling in England. She became very hostile and told Mrs Thomas not to visit any more.

Mrs Thomas then asked that the children should come and stay with her in London for a few days before she returned to Sierra Leone. In reality, she intended to keep them with her and not return them to Mrs Robertson. However, when the children came to London to stay with her, she found them to be very difficult to handle. She had never looked after them herself and they were openly critical of her way of doing things: they did not like her food, they found the flat too hot and opened all the windows, they did not like being shut in, while she went out shopping, and there was nothing to play with. She was very irritated by their 'cheeky' ways, she shouted at them a good deal, and finally Mary telephoned Mrs Robertson to say how unhappy they were. When Mrs Thomas discovered this, she hit Mary, the other children joined in and John ran out into the street screaming. Mrs Thomas felt she could not handle the situation and returned all the children to Mrs Robertson.

In 1972, Mrs Robertson, the foster mother, had the children made wards of court, but Mrs Thomas was allowed access. For five years Mrs Thomas has been trying to build a satisfactory relationship with her children and, so far, has failed. As often as not, when she calls to visit, the children have already gone out, or have appointments to go out soon after her arrival. They will not speak to her civilly and the interventions of social workers do not seem to have improved matters. Dr Thomas has twice come over from Sierra Leone, and the children are friendly and receptive to him but, as soon as he returns, they are as hostile as ever to their mother.

## V Ronke

Mrs Jones who was Nigerian had separated from her husband and had been living in England for six years with her two daughters, Tunde who was doing 'A' levels and then intended to go on to teacher training, and Ronke, aged nine. Her son, aged fifteen, had returned to Nigeria the previous year to live with his father because Mrs Jones found him too much of a handful in London and was afraid he would get into bad company. Mrs Jones herself was training to be a nurse and first contacted a social work agency to ask for a holiday home for Ronke because she was left alone when her mother was on duty and was very lonely during the school holidays.

It was arranged for Ronke to spend her summer holidays with Mr and Mrs Bennett, a retired headmaster and his wife who lived in a small isolated Yorkshire village. The Bennetts had married late and had no children of their own and they were delighted to find Ronke such an intelligent and responsive little girl. At the end of the holidays the Bennetts asked Mrs Jones if Ronke could continue to stay with them and attend the local school. Mrs Jones thought this would be a wonderful opportunity and she strongly rejected the advice of the social worker in London who suggested that Ronke might grow away from her in such a rural spot and that it would be a very isolated life for her with an elderly couple. Only in order to pacify the social worker, Mrs Jones agreed that Ronke should come home for school holidays and that either she or Tunde would visit Ronke at least once a month in order not to lose contact.

The Bennetts were living on their pension with no other means and so it was agreed that Mrs Jones should pay a small sum for Ronke's maintenance and provide her with clothes. The Bennetts were rather surprised to be visited by the local social worker as they had made a private arrangement—they clearly did not think that social workers were meant to supervise respectable middle-class people like themselves! After a few months the local social worker was expressing some concern. The Bennetts had told her that Ronke was going to stay with them until she finished school. She was the only black child for miles around and the social worker was worried about the isolation in which she would grow up. Under pressure Mrs Jones agreed that Ronke should stay only long enough to complete her primary schooling and then would come back to London. However the following year Ronke was registered to attend the local secondary school in the north and the social workers were asked not to interfere both by Mrs Jones and the Bennetts.

It was six months before Mrs Jones visited Ronke and she had no idea how long the journey would take and how expensive it would be. It was not possible for her to return the same day. The Bennetts made her welcome but did not encourage her to take Ronke out or talk to her alone. They stressed how well she was doing at school and talked about all the things they were doing with her. It was clear to Mrs Jones that she could not possibly give Ronke this sort of attention and help with her school work—she thought it was really a miracle that these people wanted to look after her daughter—it was even better than if she had been able to send her to stay with her married sister at Ibadan University, because here she was not even expected to do much about the house and she was the only child, and so she received unlimited attention. She herself did not feel very much at ease in the house—and she was glad to leave as soon as possible next morning, and to escape back to London from this very 'white' environment. Ronke seemed very happy to see her go and the Bennetts felt relieved that they had done their duty but now they were on their own again with nobody interfering.

As Ronke grew, the Bennetts were beginning to find life more and more expensive. They were buying Ronke's clothes themselves because they did not like the rather fancy things that Mrs Jones had sent, so they did ask if she would increase her payments to a realistic figure. Mrs Jones was angry—'they want her and they want my money as well', she said—and when Ronke came home for Christmas her mother visited the local school and arranged that she should start there at Easter. Mrs Jones was annoyed because Ronke complained about her food and was unwilling to do any cleaning or washing up as a twelve year old child should. Ronke was bored—there was nothing to do, no books or toys in her mother's flat, she had no friends here and her mother was too busy to take her out. She sulked and stayed in bed and when her mother smacked her, she telephoned the Bennetts, sobbing her eyes out and begging to go 'home'. Next day Mrs Bennett came and fetched her, to the relief of all parties. No more was said about increasing the contributions. Although Tunde made one visit, no further encouragement was given either for the mother to visit Yorkshire or for Ronke to go to London. Mrs Jones would have liked to feel welcome but she felt that as the Bennetts were educating her daughter so well she had better leave them to it.

When the summer holidays came round, Mrs Jones asked that Ronke should come for two weeks. Ronke wrote back and said she was 'an English girl' now, and did not want to live with black people. At Christmas she returned the presents that Tunde and her mother had sent. Mrs Jones, feeling that the situation was getting beyond her control, made another attempt to visit in the company of her sister who had just arrived from Nigeria and naturally wanted to see Ronke. They were not welcomed by the Bennetts who refused to let them into the house and said that Ronke was playing with a friend and was not there. Mrs Jones lost her temper, screamed at the Bennetts accusing them of stealing her child; her sister screamed even louder, a scuffle began and neighbours called the police.

Since then any letters from Mrs Jones have been returned to her and no money accepted. The local social worker, when approached, explained that Ronke was extremely happy where she was and that on no account could she go back to a violent, hysterical mother where she would clearly be at risk. On two occasions the mother has attempted to see Ronke at school with the hope of taking her away. The school had been alerted to this possibility and naturally a black woman arriving was so conspicuous that they were quickly alerted. As mother arrived at the school entrance, Ronke was spirited out at the back. The whole community, taxi driver, postman, school teachers, policeman, were united to save Ronke from the barbaric existence that clearly awaited her if she went back to her mother in London, let alone Nigeria.

Mrs Jones now understands what the social worker failed to convey to her in the early stages, but feels that having rejected all advice she is on her own. Her only plan is to kidnap her daughter and one can imagine the trauma for Ronke who is now totally antagonistic to her mother, referring to her as 'that black pig', if such an attempt were ever to succeed.

The local social worker has only one real worry and that is over the age of the Bennetts—however she thinks that Ronke is such a likeable child and so popular in the area that if there was a breakdown alternative foster parents could easily be found.

## VI Comfort, Felix and Mabel Armah

The three children were all born in England and had spent over five years in care since their mother had suffered from serious depression at the time of Mabel's birth. Their father had not been traced and was believed to be in the USA and their mother, after some time in hospital, was sent home to Ghana where it was thought she might respond better to treatment. For most of the five years the children were the responsibility of two different London boroughs. Comfort and Felix were together in one children's home and Mabel was initially placed with a foster mother straight from hospital, under a different authority. It was only when Mabel was five that she was reunited in a small family group home with her brother and sister then aged seven and eight. By coincidence the social worker supervising Mabel at this stage was Ghanaian. She persuaded the two boroughs to co-operate so that the children could be together, and she naturally made a point of getting to know Comfort and Felix. She talked to them about Ghana and helped them to feel that they were Ghanaians.

On two occasions, approaches were made through official channels to see if the children could return to their mother but reports came back that she was still sick and it would be better for the children to stay where they were. Eventually a Ghanaian community worker who had heard about the children offered to meet the extended family during a visit to Ghana, and to evaluate the whole situation. The children came from a matrilineal people, and Mr Frimpong, their uncle, was the head of the family, which occupied a large three-storey house. The children's mother was there but was clearly still in a very disturbed mental state; her two older sisters were living in the house with their children and there were several other family units residing there as well as some young unmarried male relatives; in all more than twenty people.

A gathering of the family elders was called and over several days the situation was discussed in detail. When it was discovered that the children were not attending a select boarding school but were living with deprived or neglected children, the family members were unanimous in agreeing that something must be done. They knew that the children's mother could neither provide the physical care that the children needed nor earn any money to support them, but Mr Frimpong agreed to accept the overall financial responsibility and his eldest sister agreed to look after the children. At first it was proposed that the children should be split up and Comfort could live with another aunt in Accra and Felix could go to a married uncle, but the community worker pointed out that these children would have special problems of adaptation and they would need each other's support. He stressed that for the initial period at least, they must remain together. He had to explain to the family that although the children were Ghanaian, they were in many ways just like English children and would need a lot of tolerance and understanding.

Planning for the children involved all the household and many other family members who lived in the area. This was particularly important in order to avoid later jealousies when it was seen that the children were getting special treatment, such as having beds to sleep on instead of mats and having expensive English foods bought for them; it was essential that privileges should be understood and accepted.

It was about a year before the children were ready to return to Ghana, just in time for Christmas.

In the next few days they had so many new experiences that they did not have time to feel 'homesick'. The social worker was anxiously wondering how long this euphoria could last and in fact it was about five days later when the Christmas celebrations had really started that reaction set in. The immediate novelty of their new life was just beginning to wear off and the children found that they were no longer the automatic centre of attraction. Christmas in Africa is primarily a religious festival and the children were not heaped with presents and sweets; the parties were for the adults and although children attended they were expected to be in the background. They relieved their loneliness by writing long letters to their housemother and drawing lots of pictures of all the funny things around. They thought about cold December England and relished the sunshine. The phase of homesickness passed fairly rapidly and the children, at least on the surface, appeared to adapt pretty easily.

The children did well in school and this gave them greater confidence. They soon learnt to communicate in the vernacular with older family members who did not speak English and with other children; in a few months they had lost their Cockney accents and were speaking English like Ghanaians. Comfort won a scholarship to one of the best boarding schools in the country and so her future was assured. The Ghanaian Social Welfare Department supervised the children and gave the family support. They reported that the major problems were financial and out of a stretched budget the family found it very difficult to pay school fees at the private international school where all the teaching was in English, and which it was agreed would give the children the best chance of settling easily into a new system.

The children belong; they have a vast family network accepting responsibility for them; they certainly miss some of the material comforts of life in the children's home, and have far more in the way of domestic chores and duties than they would have expected, but they have a future with a secure knowledge of who they are. They could so easily, but for the efforts of two Ghanaians in England who understood what they were missing, have been just three more added to the statistics of alienated Black British.

# Suggestions for further reading

## 1 West African literature

Since the publication in 1958 of *Things Fall Apart*, a brilliant first novel by the Nigerian writer, Chinua Achebe, a tremendous amount of African literature has appeared. In the African Writers' Series, published in paperback by Heinemann, there are over 180 titles and, out of these, more than half the novels are from West Africa. There are many more from other publishing houses, including some excellent translations from the French. The following is by no means a comprehensive list, but is a selection, based not primarily on literary merit but on the insight the writer gives into West African family life and traditional society.

J. W. Abruquah, *The Catechist,* Allen & Unwin, 1965.
This is the biography of an unsuccessful Ghanaian whose sons climbed to fame. One of them went to England to study, became the headmaster of a famous school in Ghana and wrote this story of his father's struggles. It gives a good picture of the strength of traditional beliefs in witchcraft—as the Catechist himself says: 'I was a Christian who still held tenaciously to the ancestral beliefs of my people.'

Chinua Achebe, *Things Fall Apart,* Heinemann, 1958; *No Longer at Ease,* Heinemann, 1960; *Arrow of God,* Heinemann, 1964.
These three novels, of real literary merit, form a trilogy, but can be read quite independently. They give a moving picture of the breakdown of traditional life caused by the arrival of the white man, and of the pressures associated with western education.

Elechi Amadi, *The Concubine,* Heinemann, 1966; *The Great Ponds,* Heinemann, 1970.
These two books tell about village life in Eastern Nigeria at the beginning of the century. 'The Concubine' is particularly interesting for its portrait of the role of women in traditional society.

Elechi Amadi, *Sunset in Biafra,* Heinemann, 1973.
This is probably the most balanced account there is of the Civil War in Nigeria and its aftermath, and it is included because of the importance of this theme in understanding contemporary Nigeria.

Peggy Appiah, *A Smell of Onions,* Longmans, 1971.
An entertaining collection of vignettes of Ghanaian village life.

Ulli Beier, *The Origin of Life and Death,* Heinemann, 1966.
Creation myths from all over Africa, but with an emphasis on West Africa.

Bernard Dadie, *Climbie,* Heinemann, 1971.
Translated from the French, this is the story of a child growing up in the Ivory Coast. It gives a good picture of the extended family and of the toughness of school life.

Amu Djoleto, *The Strange Man,* Heinemann, 1971.
Tells of one man's upbringing in traditional Ghanaian society and of the problems he later faces, as a civil servant.

R. S. Easmon, *The Burnt Out Marriage,* Nelson, 1967.
One of the few novels there are about Sierra Leone. It paints a vivid picture of the relationships in a polygamous household, and the conflicts that arise between a progressive traditional chief and his young wife from the coast.

T. O. Echewa, *The Land's Lord,* Heinemann, 1976.
A moving, philosophical study of a missionary in Eastern Nigeria, and of his clash with traditional society.

Cyprian Ekwensi, *Survive the Peace,* Heinemann, 1976.
Ekwensi has written a number of lively novels depicting city life in Nigeria. This particular book is about the confusion after the Civil War: of the breakdown in behaviour patterns and of traditions still maintained. It is a well-written novel, with a most authentic ring.

Buchi Emecheta, *In the Ditch,* Barrie & Jenkins, 1972; *Second-Class Citizen,* Alison & Busby, 1974; Fontana, 1977.
These two books portray the problems of life in England as experienced by the Nigerian author, with immense humour and disturbing comments on British attitudes. They should be read by all social workers.

Buchi Emecheta, *The Bride Price,* Alison & Busby, 1976.
Tells the story of a girl growing up in Eastern Nigeria. The writing is lively, and always interesting, but it is worth noting that some Nigerians think that Emecheta takes an exaggeratedly feminist view of the faults of her fellow countrymen.

Chukwuemeka Ike, *Toads for Supper,* Harvill Press and Fontana, 1965.
An entertaining account of the amorous adventures of a Nigerian undergraduate. In a lighthearted way it gives considerable insight into village life in Eastern Nigeria, and into the inevitable conflicts facing the educated young man.

Chukwuemeka Ike, *The Potter's Wheel,* Harvill Press, 1973.
Describes Ibo village life in the 1940s, and is particularly good on schooling.

S. A. Konadu, *A Woman in her Prime,* Heinemann, 1967.
The problem of barrenness is the principle theme explored in this novel, set in Ghana.

Camara Laye, *The African Child,* Collins, 1955; Fontana, 1959.
A beautifully written evocation of childhood and adolescence in Guinea, translated from the French. The author's father was a goldsmith who was believed to possess supernatural powers, and Laye grew up in a world where good and evil spirits were a reality. Eventually, he was drawn away from the traditional life to attend technical college in the capital, and later to study in France.

Suggestions for further reading

John Munonye, *The Only Son,* Heinemann, 1966.
This tells of a Nigerian boy brought up and spoilt by his widowed mother, and the clashes that arise when he joins the mission school.

John Munonye, *Obi,* Heinemann, 1969.
A book again dealing with the problem of barrenness, and also with the conflict between traditional religious beliefs and Christianity.

Abioseh Nicol, *The Truly Married Woman, and Other Stories,* Oxford University Press, 1965.
An excellent collection of short stories, from Sierra Leone.

Charles Njoku, *The New Breed,* Longman, 1973.
Set at the time of independence, this is a tale of a boy growing up in Eastern Nigeria.

Flora Nwapa, *Efuru,* Heinemann, 1966; *Idu,* Heinemann, 1970; *This is Lagos, and Other Stories,* Lagos, Nwankwo Ifejuka, 1971.
One of the few women writers, Nwapa is concerned with woman's role in traditional society, and also in modern Nigerian society.

E. N. Obiechina, *Onitsha Market Literature,* Heinemann, 1972.
An anthology of popular pamphlet literature, which gives an unusual glimpse of contemporary attitudes and social life, in urban Eastern Nigeria.

Francis Selormey, *The Narrow Path,* Heinemann, 1966.
The story of a teacher's son growing up in Ghana, with emphasis on the harsh discipline and strictness of school life.

Rems Nna Umeasiegbu, *The Way We Lived,* Heinemann, 1969.
A fascinating collection of customs and traditional tales from Eastern Nigeria.

## 2 Books about West Africa suitable for children

*Non-fiction*

A. A. Acquaye, *Children of West Africa,* Sterling, 1968.
A documentary account of the different life styles of children from urban and rural environments, with sections on ceremonies, schools, religion, health and play.

R. Clayton and J. Miles, *Western Africa,* Rupert Hart-Davis, 1972.
A slim, easily-read geography text book, suitable for older children and adults.

B. and P. Coard, *Getting to Know Ourselves,* Bogel L'Ouverture, 1972.
A colouring book of African and Caribbean history for very young children.

*Encyclopedia of Africa,* MacDonald, 1976.
An excellent illustrated encyclopedia in one volume, suitable as a reference book for older children and adults.

A. Goldin, *Straight Hair, Curly Hair,* Black, 1968.
A factual book in the 'Let's Look and Find Out' series.

C. Latchen, *Looking at Nigeria,* Black, 1976.
A picture book for all ages.

P. Showmers, *Your Skin and Mine,* Black, 1967.
Another book in the 'Let's Look and Find Out' series.

J. W. Watson, *Nigeria—Republic of a Hundred Kings,* Muller, 1970.
A good, lively introduction for older children.

*Fiction*

Peggy Appiah, *Tales of an Ashanti Father,* Deutsch, 1967; *The Pineapple Child,* Deutsch, 1969.
Two excellent collections of folk-tales from Ghana.

K. Arnott, *African Myths and Legends,* Oxford University Press, 1962.
Folk tales from all over Africa, but the majority from West Africa.

F. French, *Aio the Rainmaker,* Oxford University Press, 1975.

K. Kay, *Treasure Chamber,* Heinemann, 1971.

M. Owusu, *The Story Ananse Told,* Heinemann, 1971.
Three popular story books.

### 3 Social work with West Africans

Commonwealth Students' Children Society, Report of Ibadan seminar on the African child in Great Britain, 1975.

Community Relations Commission, *Fostering Black Children,* 1975.
A policy document on the needs of ethnic minority group children, with a section on those from West Africa.

Community Relations Commission, *Afro Hair and Skin Care,* 1976.
One frequent cause of friction between parents and white foster parents is hair and skin care of black children. This booklet gives sensible information and advice.

J. Ellis, 'The Fostering of West African Children in England', *Social Work Today,* vol. 2, no. 5, 1971.
A discussion of why West Africans are likely to turn to fostering for their children.

R. Holman, *Trading in Children,* Routledge & Kegan Paul, 1973.
This first study of private fostering contains a wealth of data comparing privately fostered children with those fostered by local authorities. 60 per cent of the sample of more than a hundred children were West African.

J. Jahn, *Through African Doors—Experiences and Encounters in West Africa,* New York, Grove Press, 1962.
Although this is not about social work, but is a remarkable account of a journey through West Africa, it is helpful in showing how a European was able to immerse himself in African life, and to portray his experiences with respect and love. It is also tremendously entertaining!

P. Jones-Quartey, 'Problem Solving in Ghana', *Case Conference,* vol. 14, no. 2, 1967.
A brief look at casework and West African values.

## Suggestions for further reading

D. Milner, *Children and Race,* Harmondsworth, Penguin, 1975.

A psychology book concerned with the development of children's racial attitudes and with the effects of prejudice on black children.

T. Ogbuibe, 'Children of West African Students', *Social Work Today,* vol. 3, no. 7, 1972.

A West African social worker asks how far fostering in Britain is comparable to fostering in West Africa, and examines some of the problems that arise in Britain.

J. P. Triseliotis (ed.), *Social Work with Coloured Immigrants and their Families,* Oxford University Press, 1972.

The article by Bessie Kent, 'The Social Worker's Cultural Pattern as it Affects Casework with Immigrants', is of particular interest. Although not specifically concerned with West Africans, much of what she writes about possible areas of cultural conflict has relevance to work with West Africans.

# Useful addresses

**Commonwealth Students' Children Society**

4 Cambridge Terrace,
London NW1
Telephone 01-487 3444
A voluntary society founded in 1961 by Mr B. B. Boateng to help fellow students with the many difficulties they encountered in the UK. The society works closely with local authorities and non-statutory agencies as well as making its own provisions for child-care and accommodation.

**Commission for Racial Equality**

10/12 Elliot House,
Allington Street,
London SW1
Telephone 01-828 7022
Has replaced the Community Relations Commission and the Race Relations Board.

**High Commissions**

*Ghana*

13 Belgrave Square,
London, SW1
Telephone 01-235 4142

*Nigeria*

9 Northumberland Avenue,
London WC2
Telephone 01-839 1244

*Sierra Leone*

33 Portland Place,
London W1
Telephone 01-636 6483

**International Social Service of Great Britain**

39 Brixton Road,
London SW9
Telephone 01-582 9802

This organization is especially useful if it is necessary to try and make contact with workers or families in West Africa.

**United Kingdom Council for Overseas Student Affairs**

60 Westbourne Grove,
London W2
Telephone 01-229 9268
Will give help and advice on a range of student problems including difficulties over grants.

# Bibliography


Abruquah, J. W., *The Catechist,* Allen & Unwin, 1965.

Achebe, C., *Things Fall Apart,* Heinemann, 1958.

Achebe, C. *No Longer at Ease,* Heinemann, 1960.

Achebe, C., *Arrow of God,* Heinemann, 1964.

Achebe, C., interviewed in D. Duerden and C. Pieterse, *African Writers Talking,* Heinemann, 1975.

Acquaye, A. A., *Children of West Africa,* Sterling, 1968.

Adamson, G., *The Care-Takers,* Bookstall Publications, 1973.

Amadi, E., *The Concubine,* Heinemann, 1966.

Amadi, E., *The Great Ponds,* Heinemann, 1970.

Amadi, E., *Sunset in Biafra,* Heinemann, 1973.

Appiah, P., *Tales of an Ashanti Father,* Deutsch, 1967.

Appiah, P., *The Pineapple Child,* Deutsch, 1969.

Appiah, P., *A Smell of Onions,* Longmans, 1971.

Arnott, K. *African Myths and Legends,* Oxford University Press, 1962.

Azu, G., *The Ga Family and Social Change,* Leiden, Afrika-Studiecentrum; Cambridge, African Studies Centre, 1973.

Baeta, C. G., 'Aspects of Religion', in W. Birmingham *et al.* (eds), *A Study of Contemporary Ghana,* vol. 2, Allen & Unwin, 1967.

Beier, U., *The Origin of Life and Death,* Heinemann, 1966.

Bing, G., *Reap the Whirlwind,* MacGibbon & Kee, 1968.

Caldwell, J. C., 'Population: General Characteristics'; and 'Population Prospects and Policy', in W. Birmingham *et al.* (eds), *A Study of Contemporary Ghana,* vol. 2, Allen & Unwin, 1967.

Clayton, R. and Miles, J., *Western Africa,* Rupert Hart-Davis, 1972.

Coard, B. and P., *Getting to Know Ourselves,* Bogle L'Ouverture, 1972.

Commonwealth Students' Children Society, Report of Ibadan seminar on the African child in Great Britain, 1975.

Community Relations Commission, *Fostering Black Children,* 1975.

Community Relations Commission, *Who Minds? A Study of Working Mothers and Childminding in Ethnic Minority Communities,* 1975.

Community Relations Commission, *Afro Hair and Skin Care,* 1976.

Conton, W., *The African,* Heinemann, 1960.

Craven, A., *West Africans in London,* Institute of Race Relations, 1968.

Dadie, B., *Climbie,* Heinemann, 1971.

Daniel, W. W., *Racial Discrimination in England,* Harmondsworth, Penguin, 1968.

Djoleto, A., *The Strange Man,* Heinemann, 1971.

Easmon, R. S., *The Burnt-Out Marriage,* Nelson, 1967.

Echewa, T. O., *The Land's Lord,* Heinemann, 1976.

Ellis, J., 'Child-Training in Ghana, with Particular Reference to the Ga Tribe', MA thesis, University of Ghana, 1968.

Ellis, J., 'The Fostering of West African Children in England', *Social Work Today,* vol. 2, no. 5, 1971.

Ellis, J., 'Differing Conceptions of a Child's Needs: Some Implications for Social Work with West African Children and their Parents', *British Journal of Social Work,* vol. 7, no. 2, 1977.

Ekwensi, C., *Survive the Peace,* Heinemann, 1976.

Emecheta, B., *In the Ditch,* Barrie & Jenkins, 1972.

Emecheta, B., *Second-Class Citizen,* Allison & Busby, 1974.

Emecheta, B., *The Bride-Price,* Allison & Busby, 1976.

Encyclopedia of Africa, MacDonald, 1976.

Fadipe, N. A., *Sociology of the Yoruba,* Ibadan University Press, 1970.

Fage, J. D., *An Introduction to the History of West Africa,* Cambridge University Press, 1962, 3rd edn.

Fiawoo, D. K., 'The concept of Child-Fostering in Ghana', Commonwealth Students' Children Society, Report of Ibadan seminar on the African child in Great Britain, 1975.

Field, M. J., *Social Organization of the Ga People,* Crown Agents for the Colonies, 1940.

Field, M. J., *Search for Security,* Faber & Faber, 1960.

Forde, C. D. (ed.), *African Worlds: Studies in the Cosmological Ideas and Social Values of African Peoples,* Oxford University Press, 1963.

Fortes, M., *The Web of Kinship among the Tallensi,* Oxford University Press, 1949.

Fortes, M., 'Kinship and Marriage among the Ashanti', in A. R. Radcliffe-Brown, and D. Forde (eds), *African Systems of Kinship and Marriage,* Oxford University Press, 1950.

*Foster Care—A Guide to Practice,* HMSO, 1976.

Freeman, M. D. A., *The Children Act 1975. Text with Concise Commentary,* Sweet & Maxwell, 1976.

French, F., *Aio the Rainmaker,* Oxford University Press, 1975.

Goldin, A., *Straight Hair, Curly Hair,* Black, 1968.

Goldstein, J., Freud, A. and Solnit, A. J., *Beyond the Best Interests of the Child,* Free Press, Collier-MacMillan, 1973.

Goody, E. M. and Muir, C. L., 'Factors Related to the Delegation of Parental Roles among West Africans in London', unpublished report, Committee for the Social and Political Sciences, University of Cambridge, 1972.

Green, M., *Ibo Village Affairs,* Cass, 1964.

Green, M., 'Land Tenure in an Ibo Village', quoted in E. I. Nwogugu, *Family Law in Nigeria,* Ibadan, Heinemann, 1974.

*Guardian* 'Judge lifts veil on children', 27 January 1977.

Harrell-Bond, B. E., *Modern Marriage in Sierra Leone,* The Hague, Mouton, 1975.

Holman, R., *Trading in Children,* Routledge & Kegan Paul, 1973.

Hurd, G., 'Education' in W. Birmingham *et al.* (eds), *A Study of Contemporary Ghana,* vol. 2, Allen & Unwin, 1967.

Ike, C., *Toads for Supper,* Harvill Press and Fontana, 1965.

Ike, C., *The Potter's Wheel,* Harvill Press, 1973.

Jahn, J., *Muntu,* Faber & Faber, 1961.

Jahn, J., *Through African Doors—Experiences and Encounters in West Africa,* New York, Grove Press, 1962.

Jibowu, D., 'Concepts of Motherhood', Commonwealth Students' Children Society, Report of Ibadan seminar on the African child in Great Britain, 1975.

Jones-Quartey, P., 'Problem Solving in Ghana', *Case Conference,* vol. 14, no. 2, 1967.

Kay, K., *Treasure Chamber,* Heinemann, 1971.

Kaye, B., *Bringing up Children in Ghana,* Allen & Unwin, 1962.

Kent, B., 'The Social Workers' Cultural Pattern as it Affects Casework with Immigrants', in J. P. Triseliotis (ed.), *Social Work with Coloured Immigrants and their Families,* Oxford University Press, 1972.

Kingsley, M. *Travels in West Africa,* Cass, 1965, 3rd ed.

Konadu, S. A., *A Woman in her Prime,* Heinemann, 1967.

Latchen, C., *Looking at Nigeria,* Black, 1976.

Laye, C., *The African Child,* Fontana, 1959.

Leis, P. E., *Enculturation and Socialization in an Ijaw Village,* New York, Holt, Rinehart & Winston, 1972.

Lloyd, B. B., 'Education and Family Life in the Development of Class Identification among the Yoruba', in P. C. Lloyd (ed.), *The New Elites of Tropical Africa,* Oxford University Press, 1966.

Lloyd, P. C., *Africa in Social Change,* Harmondsworth, Penguin, 1967.

Lloyd, P. C., *Power and Independence: Urban African's Perception of Social Inequality,* Routledge & Kegan Paul, 1974.

London Council of Social Service, *Child Minding in London,* 1977.

Lukes, S., *Individualism,* Oxford, Basil Blackwell, 1973.

Mabogunje, T., 'The Legal Status of Women in Africa', Commonwealth Students' Children Society, Report of Ibadan seminar on the African child in Great Britain, 1975.

Maclean, U., *Magical Medicine: A Nigerian Case-Study,* Allen Lane, The Penguin Press, 1971.

McWhinnie, A., 'The Role of the Social Services', Commonwealth Students' Children Society, Report of Ibadan seminar on the African child in Great Britain, 1975.

McWilliam, H. O. A., *The Development of Education in Ghana,* Accra, Longmans, 1964.

Marris, P., *Family and Social Change in an African City,* Routledge & Kegan Paul, 1961.

Milner, D., *Children and Race,* Harmondsworth, Penguin, 1975.

Munyone, J., *The Only Son,* Heinemann, 1966.

Munyone, J., *Obi,* Heinemann, 1969.

Nicol, A., *The Truly Married Woman, and Other Stories,* Oxford University Press, 1965.

Njoku, C., *The New Breed,* Longman, 1973.

Nukunya, G. K., *Kinship and Marriage among the Anlo Ewe,* Athlone Press, 1969.

Nwapa, F., *Efuru,* Heinemann, 1966.

Nwapa, F., *Idu,* Heinemann, 1970.

Nwapa, F., *This is Lagos, and Other Stories,* Lagos, Nwankwo Ifejuka, 1971.

Nwogugu, E. I., *Family Law in Nigeria,* Ibadan, Heinemann, 1974.

Obiechina, E. N., *Onitsha Market Literature,* Heinemann, 1972.

Obiechina, E. N., *Culture, Tradition and Society in the West African Novel,* Cambridge University Press, 1975.

Ogbuibe, T., 'Children of West African Students', *Social Work Today,* vol. 3, no. 7, 1972.

Ogunsheye, F. A., 'Formal Education and the Status of Women in Nigeria', presented at the national conference on Nigerian women and development, Ibadan, Nigeria, 1976.

Oppong, C., *Marriage among a Matrilineal Elite,* Cambridge University Press, 1974.

Owusu, M., *The Story Ananse Told,* Heinemann, 1971.

Robertson, C., 'Ga Women and Socio-Economic Change in Accra, Ghana', in N. G. Hafkin and E. G. Bay (eds), *Women in Africa, Studies in Social and Economic Change,* California, Stanford University Press, 1976.

Rowe, J. and Lambert, L., *Children Who Wait,* Association of British Adoption Agencies, 1973.

Sears, R., Maccoby, E. and Levin, H., *Patterns of Child-Rearing,* Evanston, Illinois Row, Peterson, 1957.
Selormey, F., *The Narrow Path,* Heinemann, 1966.
Showmers, P., *Your Skin and Mine,* Black, 1967.
Smith, E. W., *Aggrey of Africa,* SCM Press, 1929.
Stapleton, P., 'Culture Clashes and the childminder', *Social Work Today,* vol. 7 no. 9, 1976.
Tetteh, P. A., 'Marriage, Family and Household', in W. Birmingham *et al.* (eds) *A Study of Contemporary Ghana,* vol. 2, Allen & Unwin, 1967.
*The Times* (law report), 'African girl, 9, to remain with foster parents', 4 Decembe 1972.
*The Times* (law report), 'Foster parents to keep Ghanaian girl', 26 February 1973.
Triseliotis, J. P. (ed.), *Social Work with Coloured Immigrants and their Families* Oxford University Press, 1972.
Turnbull, C. T., *Man in Africa,* Newton Abbot, David & Charles, 1976.
Tutuola, A., *The Palm-Wine Drinkard,* Faber & Faber, 1952.
Uchendu, V. C., *The Ibo of Southeast Nigeria,* New York, Holt, Rinehart & Winston 1965.
Uka, N., *Growing up in Nigerian Culture,* Ibadan University Press, 1966.
Umeasiegbu, R. U., *The Way We Lived,* Heinemann, 1969.
United Kingdom Overseas Students' Association, *The Situation of Married Overseas Students in the UK,* pilot study, 1972.
Ware, H., 'The Changing African Family in West Africa', Commonwealth Students Children Society, Report of Ibadan seminar on the African child in Great Britain 1975.
Watson, J. W., *Nigeria—Republic of a Hundred Kings,* Muller, 1970.
Wolff, S., *Children Under Stress,* Harmondsworth, Penguin, 1973.